T0087600

Contraception and Persecution

More Titles of Interest from St. Augustine's Press

Contraception and Persecution

Charles E. Rice

Introduction by Alyssa Bormes
Preface by Steve Mosher

ST. AUGUSTINE'S PRESS
South Bend, Indiana

Manufactured in the United States of America

2 3 4 5 6   20 19 18 17 16 15

Library of Congress Control Number: 2014935185

∞ The paper used in this publication meets the minimum requirements of
the American National Standard for Information Sciences Permanence of
Paper for Printed Materials, ANSI Z39.481984.

ST. AUGUSTINE'S PRESS
www.staugustine.net

To my wife, Mary,
and
each of our children and grandchildren.

CONTENTS

INTRODUCTION

It was November 1, 2013 when my cousin posted a question on Facebook wondering where all the children were? She was perplexed by the lack of trick-or-treaters the night before. Other posts followed, saying things like, "When we were kids, the neighborhoods were filled; we got as much candy as we could." There were a number of other posts saying, "We didn't have many kids at our door last night either. I wonder why?" At my own home, I have probably had ten trick-or-treaters in the last five years combined. Perhaps candy seeking doesn't have the same appeal it used to. Or, perhaps there is something else at work.

As a child, I was one of 29 first cousins who all lived within a four or five block radius. Most other families had five to twelve kids. A friend's family only had four children, but it was explained to us that she had four brothers in heaven. There were children everywhere. But the neighborhood began to change. Families with two and three children moved in. When they heard how many children the surrounding families had, they would say things like, "We could never do that. We're done. Don't you Catholics know how to turn it off?" My little girl mind wondered how they knew they were done? What had they shut off? And what did big families have to do with Catholics, because some of the big families weren't Catholic?

What began to happened in my neighborhood when I was little, and what has happened in nearly every neighborhood since is simple – contraception.

There is an easy answer to my cousin's question about where all the children are. The answer is that the children are not – they were never allowed entry to the world, or the womb. However, if in response to her post, I answered, "Contraception," it would have been met with virtual eye rolling. I don't blame her; I was once among the eye rollers. I once thought that contraception was just a way to make marriages better – well, even if you weren't married – sex was better because it had no consequences. Well, you might get a disease, or maybe get pregnant, but there are medications for one and abortion for the other. But at least contraception allowed you to have fun. Except that it just wasn't fun anymore. Really, it was never fun. But back to the point, contraception as a reason for no trick-or-treaters? You're crazy.

My journey back to the Church began to teach me how to think, how to see the interconnectedness of seemingly disparate things. The mysterious ache in my soul that couldn't possibly have anything to do with a life of promiscuity suddenly released its hold on me when I confessed it. The cold, dark suicidal thoughts that couldn't possibly have anything to do with having killed my two children through abortion released its grip during that same confession. Studying the Church and Her teachings only helped with the healing. I finally began to see the connections. There were other sorrows in my life, but the full force of the sorrow began with my use of contraception.

I no longer roll my eyes when hearing voices for life speaking of the ills of contraception. Instead, I see the connections. In his book, *Contraception and Persecution*, Professor Charles E. Rice makes the connections between contraception and the most pressing issues of the day. Rice does not mince words when he speaks of the dictatorship of relativism, institutionalized "moral neutrality," the healthcare mandate, marriage and more. His ability to simply present arguments, and to logically stack the arguments one atop the other made me catch my breath. You might even say that Rice punched me in the gut a couple of times.

Rice quotes Pope Emeritus Benedict XVI, "We are not some casual and meaningless product of evolution. Each of us is the result of a thought of God. Each of us is willed, each of us is loved, each of us in necessary." Benedict said this at his Installation Mass. Why was this a punch in the gut to me? I was there at the

Mass. By a gift of wild providence, I had tickets with the minor diplomats. Right before the homily, we were given booklets in which the homily had been translated into many languages. When Benedict said it, it was as if all the *connections* had finally come together. I was willed, my children were willed, *every* child was willed. Every child *is* willed.

In what is one of the most shocking chapters, Rice speaks about the failure of Catholic clergy to teach *Humanae Vitae*. Then he lays out its consequences. But Rice doesn't just make the connections and leave you shaking your head, hanging it in defeat. Instead, Rice gives you hope. He calls all of us to put our shoulders back, have no fear of the connections, have no fear of the persecutions, and to get on with it. In the past, *Humanae Vitae* may not have been taught boldly in all places, but now it must be.

The world has seen many dark times; this is a dark time. But God provides lights, lanterns that light the pathway. In *Contraception and Persecution*, Charles Rice has provided such a lantern. He invites us to become lanterns, which aid in lighting the dark night. Perhaps our lanterns will bring back the nights when the multitude of children joyfully lit up the night seeking candy as a way of saying they don't fear death, instead they love *life!*

Alyssa Bormes is assistant to the President of the American Chesterton Society and author of *The Catechism of Hockey*.

PREFACE

I was an anthropologist before I became a Catholic, by which point I had realized that "the Study of Man"—the literal meaning of the word anthropology—had little to say about the really big questions: What is God? What is Man? What is the State? What is the relationship among the three? Academic anthropology's logically incoherent theories reduced God to reified man (Emile Durkheim), reduced man himself to the level of a jibbering ape (Charles Darwin), and left state power to grow unchecked (Karl Marx, followed by Vladimir Lenin, Mao Zedong, Pol Pot, etc.).

It turned out, however, that there was another anthropology, this one taught by the Catholic faith. This Christocentric anthropology, I came to learn, was part of a theoretical edifice of breathtaking scope and tremendous explanatory ability. Or as Pope Francis put it in *Lumen Fidei*, "The light of faith is unique, since it is capable of illuminating every aspect of human existence." (*Lumen Fidei*, 4)

This understanding of Man begins with God, the Creator of all things (including Man), who continued to manifest His creative power down through history by creating the souls of tens of billions of individual men and women. For most of the Christian era, state power has been checked from above by an awareness of the existence of a higher power, and from below by a shared understanding of the infinite worth of Man himself, and by the families and communities that he voluntarily forms.

The book you are now holding is illuminated by, indeed suffused with, the light of this faith, which alone enables us to see things as they really are. As such it gives us a chillingly accurate portrayal of the current American situation, in which the consciences of individual Catholics, no less than the institutional Church itself, are under a multipronged attack from the Leviathan State. Those who preach tolerance are totalitarians at heart, and they are well along—further along than most of us suspect—in capturing the institutions of power and imposing their will on people of faith.

Prof. Charles Rice ably summarizes the immediate threats to our consciences and our Church: the Health Care Mandate stemming from Obamacare, the mainstreaming of homosexuality in America, and the defection of the majority of the U.S. Supreme Court on the question of same-sex "Marriage." These are the topics of the day, and his able explanation of these errors in terms of Catholic teaching and legal doctrine will help to equip you for conversations with friends and neighbors.

Those who look to the U.S. Constitution to shield us from the tsunami of secularism that has engulfed us will surely be disappointed, in the opinion of this noted constitutional scholar. "No charter of government can survive the erosion of the culture that gave it birth," Prof. Rice affirms. "The Founders of the American republic tried to make it Christian without the Church. The system worked for a time because it drew upon the capital inherited from pre-Reformation Catholic Christendom." That capital is now gone.

The pivotal moment in its erosion, he argues in the final section of this fine book, came with the widespread acceptance of contraception by Christians, including Catholics. The connection between contraception and the Constitution, much less between contraception and the unfolding persecution of Catholics is hardly obvious. But it is nonetheless real. And Prof. Rice makes the argument as clearly as it has ever been made.

I had long understood that contraception involves the deliberate rejection of God's creative power, a spurning of His gift of life. I often said to my wife, during our childbearing years, that I wouldn't want to get to Heaven and find out that He had wanted to send us another child but that we, in our selfishness, had rejected the opportunity to cooperate with God in the creation of an immortal soul. We therefore decided to use Natural Family Planning to conceive and bear as many children as possible. (For those of you who are curious, the number that He chose to send us was nine, along with three more who preceded us to the other side.)

It was also clear to me that the fruits of contraception were undeniably bad. Contraception was merely the anteroom to an abyss of horrors the depths of which we still have not completely plumbed. Once we decided that we were "free" to reject God's gift of life, we began mutilating ourselves by sterilization, aborting our innocent unborn children, and euthanizing our helpless elderly.

We have gotten very good at numbing our God-given consciences and destroying human life.

But it was in reading Professor Rice that I understood for the first time how the massive, almost universal practice of contraception in America has opened the way for a massive assault by the State upon our liberties. By rejecting the authority of God to send us children, we have displaced Him from the very center of our lives. The State, seeing that its subjects now lack a central moral authority, immediately seeks to fill this vacuum by making a god of itself.

But this brief summary does not do this gem of a book justice. You will come away from its pages understanding that contraception is indeed the prelude to persecution.

Read on.

Steven W. Mosher is the President of the Population Research Institute and the author of numerous books on China, East Asia, and population issues.

ACKNOWLEDGMENTS

First: *Deo gratias*

This book has seen the light of day through the efforts of three people. My wife, Mary, is much loved and more than ever "the brains of the outfit" and especially of the marriage. Her encouragement and perceptive analyses were essential in the development of the manuscript. Ellen Rice is our daughter and also a professional editor and technical writer. She moonlighted efficiently for many hours on the research and editing that made this book possible. Kathleen Rice, also our daughter and a lawyer, proofread the finished manuscript meticulously and exorcised the devils lurking in the details.

We are all grateful to Bruce, Laila, and Benjamin Fingerhut for their friendship and for their unhesitating commitment of St. Augustine's Press to this project. Bruce somehow kept the whole thing on track.

I offer thanks to Alyssa Bormes and Steve Mosher for their generous preface and introduction. Alyssa exemplifies in a special way the theme of this book. On the entire international scene, Steve is the foremost lay exponent of the sanctity of innocent life and the family as defined in the teachings of the Church. And Alyssa and Steve have validated their witness by personal courage.

ABBREVIATIONS

In this book abbreviations are often used in the footnotes for frequently cited sources. In all quotations in this book, all indicated emphases are in the original documents unless otherwise noted.

CA   John Paul II, *Centesimus Annus* (1991)

C *in* V Benedict XVI, *Caritas in Veritate* (2009)

CCC   *Catechism of the Catholic Church* (1997)

DCE   Benedict XVI, *Deus Caritas Est* (2006)

EA   John Paul II, Apostolic Exhortation *Ecclesia in America* (1999)

EV   John Paul II, *Evangelium Vitae* (1995)

FC   John Paul II, *Familiaris Consortio* (1981)

FR   John Paul II, *Fides et Ratio* (1998)

HV   Paul VI, *Humanae Vitae* (1968)

LF   Pope Francis, *Lumen Fidei* (2013)

LTF   John Paul II, *Letter to Families* (1994)

ST   St. Thomas Aquinas, *Summa Theologica*

VS   John Paul II, *Veritatis Splendor* (1993)

PART I: PERSECUTION UNDER WAY

1. A PRELIMINARY BOUT:
THE HEALTH CARE MANDATE

Speaking . . . to . . . priests . . . I was trying to express
in overly dramatic fashion what the complete secularization of our society could bring. . . . I am (correctly)
quoted as saying that I expected to die in my bed, my
successor will die in prison and his successor will die a
martyr in the public square. What is omitted from the
reports is a final phrase I added about the bishop who
follows a possibly martyred bishop: "His successor will
pick up the shards of a ruined society and slowly help
rebuild civilization, as the church has done so often in
human history."—Cardinal Francis George, O.M.I.,
Archbishop of Chicago[1]

As Cardinal George noted, the Church has a way of outlast-
ing persecutions and bringing from them a greater good. That
record is now put to the test on a larger scale than it was in
Rome in the first three centuries. "So many Christian communities are persecuted around the globe," said Pope Francis. "More
so now than in the early times."[2] Archbishop Silvano Tomasi,
Observer of the Holy See to the UN, recently told the UN
Human Rights Council that "more than 100,000 Christians are

---

1   *The Cardinal's Column, Catholic New World,* Oct. 21-Nov. 3, 2012; see
    Tim Drake, "The Myth and the Reality of 'I'll Die in My Bed,'" *National
    Catholic Register,* Oct. 24, 2012.
2   Pope Francis, Homily at Santa Marta, May 4, 2013; *L'Osservatore Romano*
    (English), May 8, 2013, p. 3.

violently killed because of some relation to their faith every year."[3]

Cardinal George was optimistic in not expecting martyrdom until the successor of his successor. The persecution of the Catholic Church in the United States is already under way. Numerous government measures would restrict or silence the public ministries of the Church. Catholic adoption agencies in several states have been forced to terminate their adoption programs rather than comply with legal mandates that they place children with same-sex couples.[4] The Food and Drug Administration decreed that girls as young as fifteen can buy the abortifacient Morning After Pill without a prescription.[5] In response to a decree of a federal judge, the Obama Administration removed any age limitation on over-the-counter access to pills that can cause an abortion by preventing implantation of the embryo in the womb.[6] This undermines the authority of parents and the teaching of the Church on the right to life. President Obama and his Administration promote the homosexualization of American law and culture, including especially the legalization of same-sex "marriage."[7] Such an attempt to repeal Genesis ("Male and female He created them."[8]) and to homosexualize the entire culture by force of law would practically eliminate the public ministry of the Church. If the legal mandate for equality controls, could the Church legally deny a wedding ceremony to two Catholic men or two Catholic women?

The most immediate attack on the Church is the Health Care Mandate. That Mandate involves an implicit claim of the State to be God. It also presents to the Church a teaching moment on

3   LifeSiteNews.com, May 29, 2013.
4   U.S. Conference of Catholic Bishops (USCCB) Fact Sheet, "Religious Liberty Under Attack: Concrete Examples" (2013); *Today's Catholic*, June 16, 2013, p. 9.
5   LifeSiteNews.com, May 1, 2013.
6   LifeSiteNews.com, June 13, 2013; LifeSiteNews.com, April 5, 2013.
7   See Chapter 3, below.
8   Gen. 1:27

contraception[9] as well as conscience.[10] Contraception is a First Commandment issue: *Who is God?* The contracepting couple, in the words of John Paul II, "claim a power which belongs solely to God: the power to decide, in *a final analysis*, the coming into existence of a human person."[11] The nearly universal practice of contraception has paved the way for a similar assertion of divine prerogative by the Obama Regime in its claim of discretionary power to nullify the due rights of conscience. The Mandate is a preliminary event in this accelerating persecution of the Church and of believing Catholics.

The Health Care Mandate

On January 20, 2012, Health and Human Services Secretary Kathleen Sebelius, incidentally a Catholic, ordered that health insurance must cover preventive services including all FDA-approved "contraceptive" methods, including abortifacients which are called contraceptives, sterilization procedures, and patient education and counseling for all women with reproductive capacity, without charging a co-payment, co-insurance, or deductible. Catholic dioceses, hospitals, schools, church agencies and universities, as well as non-Catholic and private employers, filed lawsuits claiming that the Mandate violates the Constitution and federal laws, including the religious freedom protected by the First Amendment. As the bishops correctly insist, the suits do not themselves involve the legal status of contraception or the merits of the Church's teaching on contraception. Those suits are not resolved by the Supreme Court's upholding in July 2012 of Obamacare's Individual Mandate requiring individuals to buy health care insurance for themselves.[12]

The revision of the Mandate, in February 2013, was accurately

9   See Chapters 9–12.
10 See Chapter 6.
11 Pope John Paul II, *Discourse*, Sept. 17, 1983.
12 *National Federation of Independent Businesses v. Sebelius*, 132 S. Ct. 2566 (2012).

described by the United States Conference of Catholic Bishops (USCCB) as unacceptable:

> **The mandate is unchanged.** Almost all health plans must cover female sterilizations, all FDA-approved "contraceptives"—including drugs and devices that can prevent implantation, and at least one drug (Ella) that can cause abortion after implantation—and related "education and counseling" for women and girls of reproductive age. . . .
>
> **The "religious employer" exemption still excludes most religious organizations.** . . . Only a church, its integrated auxiliary, a convention or association of churches, or the exclusively religious activities of a religious order are exempt. . . .
>
> **The proposed "accommodation" for non-exempt religious employers does not remove the burden on religious freedom.** A wide array of religious organizations—schools, colleges, universities, hospitals, charitable agencies . . . —are not exempt.. . . . [T]heir employees (and employees' dependent female children) will be "automatically" enrolled in the mandated coverage. The "accommodation" is that arrangements for imposing this "separate" coverage, and for notifying employees about it, will be made by others—by the insurance company in the case of insured plans, by the third-party administrator in the case of self-insured plans. However, the employer is still called upon to help fund and/or facilitate the objectionable coverage.
>
> **Many with moral and religious objections remain ineligible for any exemption or "accommodation."** These include: Individual purchasers and their families; employees of religious organizations that qualify only for the "accommodation" (since these employees will still be automatically enrolled in the objectionable

coverage); for-profit companies and businesses, including those owned and controlled by religious believers; nonprofit employers who are not explicitly religious in character (e.g., pro-life groups that object to abortifacients).[13]

Later revisions of the Mandate have not resolved these difficulties.[14] Bishop Daniel Jenky, C.S.C., of Peoria, described the effect the Mandate would have on the public ministries of the Church:

> [O]ur Catholic schools, our Catholic hospitals, our Catholic Newman Centers, all our public ministries—only excepting our church buildings—could easily be shut down. Because no Catholic institution . . . can ever cooperate with . . . killing innocent human life in the womb.
>
> No Catholic ministry—and yes, Mr. President, for Catholics our schools and hospitals are ministries—can remain faithful to the Lordship of the Risen Christ and to his glorious Gospel of Life if they are forced to pay for abortion.[15]

Bishop Jenky is definitely an optimist. In a serious persecution not even the "church buildings" will be permitted to be used as "public ministries" of the Church. As Cardinal Timothy Dolan, president of the USCCB, put it, the Mandate would reduce religion to a private activity. "Never before," he said, "have we faced this kind of challenge to our ability to engage in the public square as people of faith."[16]

Religious freedom is about more than gathering in church buildings for worship. It requires freedom for "caritas," the

---

13   Statement, USCCB Secretariat of Pro-Life Activities, March 27, 2013.
14   "Standing Together for Religious Freedom," an open letter by 58 representatives of various faiths, July 2, 2013, *National Catholic News*, July 2, 2013. See statement by the United States bishops, Sept. 17, 2013.
15   Bishop Daniel R. Jenky, C.S.C., of Peoria, IL, April 14, 2012.
16   *Wall Street Journal*, Opinion, May 22, 2012.

Church's "service of charity,"[17] in its numerous manifestations, including the "commitment to justice" through the effort "to help form consciences in political life."[18] The Mandate threatens to reduce the Church to a privatized entity incapable of exercising its ministry of "caritas." The persecution of the Church, however, does not depend on the outcome of the Mandate litigation.

Effect of the Mandate Lawsuits

If the lawsuits succeed and the Supreme Court strikes down the Mandate, that result will not stop the accelerating persecution. The hostility of President Obama and his Regime is not the entire reason the Church is exposed to persecution. If Obama had never been elected, the Catholic Church and the secular State would still have been on a collision course on foundational issues of family, the transmission of life, the right to life of each human being, economic justice, and especially the many issues associated with same-sex "marriage." The Health Care Mandate requires us to reflect also on the self-imposed vulnerability of the American Catholic Church and its members to oppression by the secular elites. American Catholics and the bishops of the American Church have invited persecution by their acceptance of and, in the case of the bishops, their failure to teach about, the corrosive contraceptive mentality.[19]

If, on the other hand, the Supreme Court upholds the Health Care Mandate, we will find out the hard way how a persecution progresses. In a 2012 address at the University of Notre Dame, Archbishop Carlo Maria Viganò, Apostolic Nuncio to the United States, discussed "Religious Freedom, Persecution of the Church, and Martyrdom." Persecution can take various forms, especially in the beginning. Archbishop Viganò's analysis offers help in recognizing the early stages of persecution:

17 *Deus Caritas Est*, no. 19.
18 *Ibid.*, no. 28(a).
19 See Chapters 9–12.

There are those who question whether religion or religious belief should have a role in public life and civic affairs. . . . [P]ersecution begins with this reluctance to accept the public role of religion in these affairs, especially . . . when the protection of religious freedom involves beliefs that the powerful of the political society do not share. . . . [T]he intention . . . of the persecutor is . . . to eradicate the public witness to Jesus Christ and His Church. An accompanying objective can be the incapacitation of the faith by enticing people to renounce their beliefs, or at least their public manifestations, rather than undergo great hardships . . . if believers persist in their resistance to apostasy. The plan is straightforward: if the faith persists, so will the hardships. In more recent times, martyrdom may not necessitate torture and death; . . . those who desire to harm the faith may choose the path of ridiculing the believers so that they become outcasts from mainstream society and are marginalized from meaningful participation in public life. . . . While . . . persecution can mirror . . . martyrdom, other elements can be directed to sustaining difficulty, annoyance, and harassment that are designed to frustrate the beliefs of the targeted person or persons rather than to eliminate these persons. . . . [T]he objective of persecution is to remove from the public square the beliefs themselves and the public manifestations without necessarily eliminating the persons who hold the beliefs. The victimization may not be designed to destroy the believer but only the belief and its open manifestations. From the public viewpoint, the believer remains but the faith eventually disappears.[20]

Archbishop Viganò noted that, in the United States, "we witness in an unprecedented way a platform being assumed by a

---

20 Address, Archbishop Carlo Maria Viganò, "Religious Freedom, Persecution of the Church, and Martyrdom," Univ. of Notre Dame, Nov. 4, 2012.

major political party, having intrinsic evils among its basic principles, and Catholic faithful publicly supporting it. There is a divisive strategy at work here, an intentional dividing of the Church; through this strategy, the body of the Church is weakened, and thus the Church can be more easily persecuted." That is why the Health Care Mandate is merely a preliminary event.

2. THE UNJUST LAW: OBEY? OR WHAT?

If the Supreme Court upholds the Health Care Mandate, the fact that the Church has sued does not morally commit it to accept that outcome and obey that decree. Religious freedom is not given to us by the Constitution. It is, as the Catholic bishops and leaders of other faiths affirm, a fundamental right grounded in the nature and dignity of the human person.

No state ever has the right to violate that basic right as the Mandate does. In attempting to do so, the Regime has given to the Church a teaching moment. The bishops have preserved their ability to use that moment. As they said in a letter they ordered read in every parish in the land: "We cannot, we will not comply with this unjust law."[21] But why is that law unjust? Because it compels, contrary to conscience, cooperation with intrinsic evils—contraception and abortion.

An Unjust Law?

In an interview with Thomas McKenna, Cardinal Raymond Burke, Prefect of the Vatican's Supreme Tribunal of the Apostolic Signatura, said, "I admire very much the courage of the bishops. . . . I believe they would say it along with me that they are doing no more than their duty. A bishop has to protect his flock and when any individual or government attempts to force the flock to act against conscience in one of its most fundamental precepts then the bishops have to . . . defend those . . . entrusted to their pastoral care."

McKenna: "So a Catholic employer . . . does not provide this because . . . they would be . . . cooperating with . . . the sin of

---

21 LifeSiteNews.com, Jan. 30, 2012.

contraception or the sin of providing a contraceptive that would abort a child. Is this correct?"

Cardinal Burke: "This is correct. It is not only . . . 'material cooperation' in the sense that the employer by giving this insurance benefit is *materially providing* for the contraception but it is also 'formal cooperation' because he is *knowingly and deliberately* doing this, making this available to people. There is no way to justify it. It is simply wrong."[22]

A properly formed conscience will judge that the Mandate unjustly compels immoral cooperation with contraception and abortion.

Should You Ever Obey an Unjust Law?

In refusing to comply with the Mandate, are the bishops asserting an impossible right for the citizen to pick and choose what laws he will obey? The answer depends on the distinction, clarified by St. Thomas Aquinas, between a law that is unjust because it is contrary to "human good" and a law that is unjust because it is contrary to "Divine good" in that it compels you to violate the "Divine law."

Can you ever be morally bound to obey an unjust law? A human law, said Aquinas, that is contrary to the "law of nature" is unjust and "a perversion of law."[23] But, to avoid a greater evil, we may be morally required to obey a law which is unjust as contrary to "human good," i.e., beyond the authority of the lawgiver, oppressive, or a serious violation of equality. Any lawyer can think of injustices in the income tax laws. But we still have a duty to pay that tax.

On the other hand, "laws may be unjust through being opposed to the Divine good; such are . . . laws . . . inducing . . . to anything . . . contrary to the Divine law; and laws of this kind must nowise be observed, because, as stated in *Acts* 5:29, 'we

22 Lifesitenews.com, www.lifesitenews.com/2012/04/10.
23 *ST*, I, II, Q. 95, art. 2.

ought to obey God rather than men.'"[24] The Mandate compels a violation of "Divine law" because it compels, in the words of Cardinal Burke, "not only . . . 'material cooperation' . . . but . . . also 'formal cooperation'" with evil.[25] The bishops have no choice other than to refuse compliance.

No Compromise

How serious is this? Potentially: very. If there were no laws protecting a doctor's right of conscience on abortion and an Army doctor were ordered to perform an abortion, he would be bound to refuse even at the cost of his life. The bishops have bound themselves by the same duty to refuse immoral cooperation in a violation of the divine law. And, in principle, at whatever cost to themselves the law might impose. They are entitled to encouragement, vocal support, and, especially, prayer.

"[In the] 20th century," said John Paul II, "human consciences have been particularly violated. In the name of totalitarian ideologies, millions of people were forced to act against their deeper convictions. . . . [T]he rights of conscience must be defended today as well. In the name of tolerance, a powerful intolerance . . . is . . . spreading to public life, and in the mass media. Believers . . . notice the . . . tendency to marginalize them from the life of society: what is most sacred to them is . . . mocked and ridiculed."[26]

No person or entity on earth, *or below*, has any moral power to require persons to violate the prohibitory law of God. The Ten Commandments are specifications of the natural law.[27] The positive precepts may not apply "in view of other duties which may be more important or urgent."[28] A child is bound to obey his parents. But if they ordered him to steal he would be obliged to disobey them. "[T]he negative precepts," said John Paul II, "oblige each

24   *ST* I, II, Q. 96, art. 4.
25   www.LifeSiteNews.com/2012/04/10.
26   Pope John Paul II, Homily, May 22, 1995.
27   *VS*, no. 79.
28   *VS*, no. 67.

and every individual, always and in every circumstance . . . without exception. . . . [I]t is always possible that man . . . can be hindered from doing certain good actions; but he can never be hindered from not doing certain actions, especially if he is prepared to die rather than do evil."[29] He could have been speaking of the Health Care Mandate, an unjust law that would compel action "contrary to [a prohibition of] the Divine Law."[30]

The bishops, in short, do not need approval by the Supreme Court to affirm that "we must obey God rather than men."[31] They—and the Catholic Church—are the targets of persecution because the real conflict here is between Satan and Christ "who lives in the Church, and through her teaches, governs and sanctifies."[32]

The theory of the Mandate is that of Mexican President Plutarco Elías Calles who, to justify a bloody persecution of Catholics in the 1920s, told Bishop Pasqual Diaz, who had appealed to conscience, that: "The law is above the dictates of conscience."[33] A state that claims the right to compel people to violate a prohibition of Divine Law is claiming a power superior to that of God Himself.

The Obama Regime focuses its Health Care Mandate on contraception because the teaching on contraception is widely seen as the Achilles' heel of the Church. In truth, however, the positive, hopeful teaching on marriage and the transmission of life is one of the strongest weapons the Church has in this cultural and religious war.[34]

This crisis has been a long time in developing. It arises from the Enlightenment, the effort of politicians and philosophers, over the past three centuries and more, to build a society as if God did

29 *VS*, no. 52.
30 *ST* I, II, Q. 96, art. 4.
31 *Acts* 5:29.
32 Pope Paul VI, *Ecclesiam Suam* (1964), nos. 30, 50.
33 Carl Anderson, "Who Can Be a Priest—The Question that Killed 200,000 Mexicans," in Ruben Quezada, *For Greater Glory* (2012), 97.
34 See Chapter 13.

not exist. The key issues involve epistemology, a fifty-cent word meaning the science of knowing. "Faith and reason," said John Paul II, "are like two wings on which the human spirit rises to the contemplation of truth."[35] We are entering a period of persecution because American culture has lost not only its faith but its mind. Nowhere is their flight from faith and reason more evident than in the treatment by American law and culture of marriage, the family, and the creation of human beings as male and female.

35 *FR*, Preamble.

3. THE MAIN EVENT: A "QUEER" AMERICA?

The Health Care Mandate is a "prelim"—one of the preliminary bouts on the undercard before the main event. That main event is the bout to determine whether the United States will conform its law and culture to the homosexual lifestyle in all its aspects—Gay, Lesbian, Bisexual, Transgendered, Questioning. GLBTQ does not exhaust the foreseeable categories. That main event is well under way and GLBTQ is far ahead on points.

Parenthetically, the word "Queer" in the title of this chapter is not intended as an epithet or a caricature. Significant elements of the GLBTQ movement have adopted that term to describe their own movement. For example, the LGBT Resource Center at the University of California, Davis, in the fall of 2012, sponsored a "Queer Welcome" for new students, followed by the fourth annual "Queer Leadership Retreat." The Glossary published by the Center defines the term: "QUEER: Anyone who chooses to identify as such. This can include, but is not limited to, gays, lesbians, bisexuals, transgendered people, intersex people, asexual people, allies, leather fetishists, freaks, etc. Not all the people in the above subcategories I.D. as queer, and many people NOT in the above groups DO. This term has different meanings to different people. Some still find it offensive, while others reclaim it to encompass the broader sense of history of the gay rights movement. Can also be used as an umbrella term like LGBT, as in 'the queer community'."[36]

The homosexual movement is not at all about a right of persons to be free from unjust discrimination against them and their lifestyle. Rather, it is a totalitarian movement that demands that society and the law affirm those lifestyles not only as good but

36 www.lgbtcenter.ucdavis.edu/lgbt-education/lgbtquia-glossary.

also as entitled to special privilege even to the point of abrogating millennia of moral tradition dating back to *Genesis*. It is not enough, however, simply to oppose same-sex marriage on pragmatic or political grounds. What is needed is an understanding and fair exposition of that tradition as found in faith and reason.

Disorders: Act and Inclination

As the *Catechism* makes clear, homosexuals are entitled to respect and protection from unjust discrimination. But homosexual acts, as well as the homosexual inclination, are disordered and homosexual conduct is a moral and social evil:

> 2357 Homosexuality refers to relations between men or between women who experience an exclusive or predominant sexual attraction toward persons of the same sex. It has taken a great variety of forms through the centuries and in different cultures. Its psychological genesis remains largely unexplained. Basing itself on Sacred Scripture, which presents homosexual acts as acts of grave depravity, tradition has always declared that "homosexual acts are intrinsically disordered." They are contrary to the natural law. They close the sexual act to the gift of life. They do not proceed from a genuine affective and sexual complementarity. Under no circumstances can they be approved.

> 2358 The number of men and women who have deep-seated homosexual tendencies is not negligible. This inclination, which is objectively disordered, constitutes for most of them a trial. They must be accepted with respect, compassion, and sensitivity. Every sign of unjust discrimination in their regard should be avoided. These persons are called to fulfill God's will in their lives and, if they are Christians, to unite to the sacrifice of the Lord's Cross the difficulties they may encounter from their condition.

2359 Homosexual persons are called to chastity. By the virtues of self-mastery that teach them inner freedom, at times by the support of disinterested friendship, by prayer and sacramental grace, they can and should gradually and resolutely approach Christian perfection.

Same-Sex "Marriage"

Since Adam and Eve, marriage has always been the union of one man and one woman. God—not the State or the human law—created and defined it. The law cannot change that any more than it could make a man an aunt or a woman an uncle. "The intimate community of life and love which constitutes the married state has been established by the Creator and endowed by him with its own proper laws. . . . God himself is the author of marriage. . . . Holy Scripture affirms that man and woman were created for one another."[37]

Even if you don't believe in God, reason and common sense can help you understand what marriage is. "The family," according to Aristotle, "is the association established by nature for the supply of men's everyday wants." It is founded, he said, on "a union of those who cannot exist without each other; namely, of male and female, that the race may continue."[38] Marriage, in the words of Supreme Court Justice Stephen Field in 1888, "is something more than a mere contract . . . It is an institution, in the maintenance of which in its purity the public is deeply interested, for it is the foundation of the family and of society, without which there would be neither civilization nor progress."[39]

The law gives exclusive rights, privileges, and responsibilities, the legal "incidents" of marriage, to this union of man and woman because the spouses make a public commitment to each other, and to the community, to raise and educate any children of

37 CCC, nos. 1603, 1605; Genesis 2:24.
38 Aristotle, Politics, book I (Benjamin Jowett, transl.), in *Basic Works of Aristotle* (Richard McKeon, ed., 1941), 1127.
39 *Maynard v. Hill*, 125 U.S. 190, 210–11 (1888).

that marriage. Those commitments confer a unique benefit on society and the state.

Only a man-woman union can produce new citizens. A "gay" or lesbian couple can legally adopt a child. But they cannot produce new persons. Homosexual activity is intrinsically a dead end. It cannot give new life to the world. "Society's stake in marriage," noted Methodist Pastor Donald Sensing, is "the perpetuation of the society itself."[40]

"Because married couples ensure the succession of generations . . . civil law grants them institutional recognition. Homosexual unions . . . do not need specific attention from the legal standpoint because they do not exercise this function for the common good."[41] There is no injustice here. Cohabiting homosexual or heterosexual couples still have the legal ability to protect their rights and interests, by contracts and otherwise, without the legal recognition of their unions as equivalent or analogous to marriage.

In 2003, Cardinal Joseph Ratzinger (later Pope Benedict XVI), Prefect of the Congregation for the Doctrine of the Faith, issued *Considerations Regarding Proposals to Give Legal Recognition to Unions Between Homosexual Persons*. That document, approved by Pope John Paul II, spelled out the reasons why "[t]here are absolutely no grounds for considering homosexual unions to be in any way . . . even analogous to God's plan for marriage or family. Marriage is holy, while homosexual acts go against the moral law."[42] "Moral conscience requires," said *Considerations*, "that . . . Christians give witness to the whole moral truth, which is contradicted both by approval of homosexual acts and unjust discrimination against homosexual persons."[43] To confer the legal incidents

---

40 Donald Sensing, "Save Marriage? It's Too Late," *Wall Street Journal*, March 15, 2004, *Opinion Journal*.
41 Congregation for the Doctrine of the Faith, *Considerations Regarding Proposals to Give Legal Recognition to Unions Between Homosexual Persons* (2003), no. 9.
42 *Considerations*, no. 4.
43 *Ibid.*, no. 5.

of marriage on same-sex "civil unions" can no more be justified than the conferral of the name, "marriage," on them: "By putting homosexual unions on a legal plane analogous to that of marriage and the family, the State acts . . . in contradiction with its duties. . . . [S]uch unions are harmful to the proper development of human society, especially if their impact on society were to increase."[44]

"Legal recognition of homosexual unions or placing them on the same level as marriage would mean not only the approval of deviant behavior, with the consequence of making it a model in present-day society, but would also obscure basic values which belong to the common inheritance of humanity."[45] *Considerations* noted "the difference between homosexual behavior as a private phenomenon and the same behavior as a relationship . . . approved by the law as one of the institutions in the legal structure. . . . Civil laws . . . play a very important . . . role in influencing . . . thought and behavior. Lifestyles and the . . . presuppositions these express . . . modify the younger generation's perception and . . . behavior. Legal recognition of homosexual unions would . . . cause a devaluation of . . . marriage. . . . The denial of the . . . status of marriage to forms of cohabitation that . . . cannot be marital is not opposed to justice; on the contrary, justice requires it."[46]

Where Do You Draw the Line?

In the nature of things, a marriage between persons of the same sex is intrinsically impossible, a contradiction in terms. To ensure the perpetuation of the human race, God created a guy and a girl, named Adam and Eve. If he had started with two guys or two girls, whatever their names, the project would have gone nowhere.

If one guy can "marry" another guy, why can't they include a

44 *Ibid.*, no. 8.
45 *Ibid.*, no. 11.
46 *Ibid.*, nos. 6 and 8.

third guy in the mix? Or a third guy, a girl or two, and another guy? The legal recognition of same-sex "marriage" or civil unions would predictably extend to all the varieties of the GLBTQ culture. That would include relations amounting in effect to polygamy (one man, multiple women), polyandry (one woman, multiple men), polyamory (three or more partners where all have sexual relations with all the others), incest, and, of course, bestiality. Princeton University Professor Peter Singer, the founder of the animal rights movement, noted that, "[o]ne by one, the taboos have fallen. The idea that it could be wrong to use contraception in order to separate sex from reproduction is now merely quaint. . . . The existence of sexual contact between humans and animals, and the potency of the taboo against it, displays the ambivalence of our relationship with animals."[47] In Singer's view, commented a *Wall Street Journal* editorial, "when it comes to sex with farm animals, the only real issues are whether you get the animal's consent—and you don't kill it as part of your pleasure."[48] Interestingly, Singer seems to acknowledge that the falling of the "taboos" arose from the acceptance of contraception. But it all begins with the loss of God. "Once I think that by turning away from God I will find myself," wrote Pope Francis in his first encyclical, "my life begins to fall apart."[49]

A War on God

As John Paul II put it: "When the sense of God is lost, the sense of man is also threatened and poisoned. . . . Without the Creator the creature would disappear. . . . [W]hen God is forgotten the creature itself grows unintelligible. Man is no longer able to see himself as 'mysteriously different' from other earthly creatures; he regards himself merely as one more living being, as an organism which, at most, has reached a very high stage of perfection."[50]

47 Peter Singer, "Heavy Petting," www.nerve.com/opinions/Singer/heavypetting/.
48 *Opinion Journal*, www.wsj.com, March 30, 2001.
49 *Lumen Fidei* (2013), no. 19.
50 *EV*, no. 22.

The militant homosexual movement seeks nothing less than the destruction of the social order based on the family as instituted by God and known through reason as well as faith. Archbishop John Myers, of Newark, painted in 2006 a picture of a future we already know by experience:

> As many supporters . . . of same-sex "marriage" (or its equivalent) . . . admit, the logic of their position points to the abolition of marriage as a socially normative institution. Anyone who teaches—or preaches—that marriage is an exclusive union of one man and one woman will be labeled a bigot. Anyone who teaches—or preaches—that sexual relations between a man and a man or a woman and a woman are morally wrong will be charged with prejudice. Anyone who teaches—or preaches—that children need a mom and a dad and that two moms or two dads are not the same will be marginalized as an enemy of equality.

> And everyone knows what will soon follow: Christian, Jewish, Muslim and other religious communities will come under intense political pressure and legal attack. [And] they will be . . . vulnerable to laws prohibiting what advocates of sexual liberation . . . will insist is "discrimination."

> We have already seen this wherever same-sex relations have been given legal standing.[51]

The "gay rights" agenda mentioned by Archbishop Myers takes on an even more totalitarian cast when it is imposed by unelected judges. The 2013 rulings by the Supreme Court on same-sex marriage foreshadow a uniform, nation-wide enforcement of that agenda.[52]

---

51 36 *Origins*, Nov. 9, 2006, pp. 345–46.
52 See Chapter 4.

4. THE SUPREME COURT AND
SAME-SEX MARRIAGE

On June 26, 2013, the Supreme Court decided two cases:[53] *Hollingsworth v. Perry* involved Proposition 8, an initiative amending the California Constitution to define marriage as a union between a man and a woman. A U.S. District Court and the Court of Appeals held that Prop. 8 was unconstitutional as a violation of "gay" people's right to equal treatment. The Governor and other State officials refused to appeal that ruling. The District Court and Court of Appeals permitted the proponents of Prop. 8 to seek review by the Supreme Court of the United States of the District Court's ruling against Prop. 8.

Article III, Section 2, of the U.S. Constitution limits the judicial power of federal courts to "cases" and "controversies," which means that "the party invoking the power of the court . . . must . . . have 'standing' which requires, among other things, that it have suffered a concrete and particularized injury."[54] The Supreme Court in *Hollingsworth* held that the proponents of Prop. 8 did not have standing and it dismissed the appeal because "the District Court had not ordered [petitioners, the proponents of Prop. 8] to do or refrain from doing anything. To have standing, a litigant must seek relief for an injury that affects him in a 'personal and individual way.'"[55]

Hollingsworth practically affects only California. It therefore lacks the national significance of the *Windsor* decision.

---

53 *Hollingsworth v. Perry*, 133 S. Ct. 2652 (2013); *U.S. v. Windsor*, 133 S. Ct. 2675 (2013).
54 *Hollingsworth*, 133 S. Ct. at 2659.
55 *Ibid.*, 2662.

U.S. v. Windsor[56]

Edith Windsor and Thea Spyer, New York residents, were recognized as legally married by the law of that State. When Spyer died, she left her estate to Windsor. Windsor claimed the federal estate tax exemption as a surviving spouse. She was denied the exemption because Section 3 of the Defense of Marriage Act (DOMA) excludes a same-sex partner from the definition of "spouse" as that term is used in federal statutes. Windsor paid $363,053 in estate taxes and sued in the U.S. District Court in New York for a refund. While that suit was pending, the Attorney General stated that the Department of Justice would no longer defend the constitutionality of Section 3 of DOMA. The District Court allowed the Bipartisan Legal Advisory Group (BLAG) of the House of Representatives to intervene as an interested party to defend the constitutionality of Section 3. The Supreme Court appointed a law professor as *amicus curiae* to argue the position that the Supreme Court lacked jurisdiction to hear the case.

The Supreme Court held that it had jurisdiction. On the merits, the Court held that Section 3 is unconstitutional as a denial of the equal protection of the laws guaranteed by the Fifth Amendment.

The Court's Ruling on Jurisdiction

Public reaction to *Windsor* has focused on the Court's discussion of same-sex marriage. The ruling on jurisdiction, however, is more dangerous to the rule of law.

"The judicial Power of the United States shall be vested in one Supreme Court, and in such inferior courts as the Congress may from time to time ordain and establish."[57] Congress created the District Courts and Courts of Appeals pursuant to this authorization. "The judicial Power" exercised by those courts "shall

56 133 S. Ct. 2675 (2013).
57 Constitution, Art. III, Sec. 1.

extend" to a variety of "cases" and "controversies," including cases "arising under this Constitution [or] the Laws of the United States."[58] In the absence of a "case" or "controversy," no court created under Article III has jurisdiction. Obviously, the Supreme Court cannot hear every case or controversy presented to it for review. The Court, therefore, has discretion to make a prudential judgment as to justiciability, i.e., which cases or controversies it will actually hear.

If a matter does not present a case or controversy, the Court has no power to make a prudential judgment that it will hear that case. Yet that is what the Court did in *Windsor*. In his opinion for the Court, Justice Anthony Kennedy said: "Unlike Article III requirements—which must be satisfied by the parties before judicial consideration is appropriate—the relevant prudential factors that counsel against hearing this case are subject to 'countervailing considerations [that] may outweigh the concerns underlying the usual reluctance to exert judicial power.'. . . . One consideration is the extent to which adversarial presentation of the issues is assured by the participation of *amici curiae* . . . to defend . . . the constitutionality of the legislative act. . . . BLAG's . . . presentation of the issues satisfies the prudential concerns that otherwise might counsel against hearing an appeal from a decision with which the principal parties agree."[59]

This is an astonishing seizure of power by the Court to decide a case "in which the principal parties agree" and in which there is, therefore, no case or controversy to which "[t]he judicial power shall extend."[60] "The authorities the majority cites," wrote Justice Antonin Scalia in his dissent, "fall miles short of supporting the counterintuitive notion that an Article III 'controversy' can exist without disagreement between the parties."[61] The Supreme Court has "'prudential discretion' . . . to *deny* an appeal even when a live controversy exists—not the discretion to

58 Art III, Sec. 2.
59 133 S. Ct. at 2687–88.
60 Art. III, Sec. 2, 4.
61 133 S. Ct. at 2701.

grant one when it does not."[62] "[T]he plaintiff and the Government," he said, "agree entirely on what should happen in this lawsuit."[63]

Justice Scalia described as "jaw-dropping" the majority's assertion that "'when an Act of Congress is alleged to conflict with the Constitution, it is emphatically the province and duty of the judicial department to say what the law is.'"[64] "As Justice Brandeis put it," Scalia said, "we cannot 'pass upon the constitutionality of legislation in a friendly, non-adversary, proceeding'; absent a 'real, earnest and vital controversy between individuals,' we have neither any work to do nor any power to do it."[65] The unprecedented character of the *Windsor* ruling on jurisdiction was described by Justice Scalia:

> In the more than two centuries that this Court has existed . . . , we have never suggested that we have the power to decide a question when every party agrees with both its nominal opponent *and the court below* on that question's answer.[66]

> The question here is not whether, as the majority puts it, 'the United States retains a stake sufficient to support Article III jurisdiction,' . . . the question is whether there is any controversy (which requires *contradiction*) between the United States and Ms. Windsor. There is not.[67]

> The majority can cite no case in which this Court entertained an appeal in which both parties urged us to affirm the judgment below. . . . [T]he existence of a controversy is not a "prudential" requirement that we have

62 *Ibid.*, 2702.
63 *Ibid.*, 2698.
64 *Ibid.*, 2688, 2698.
65 *Ibid.*, 2699.
66 *Ibid.*, 2700.
67 *Ibid.*, 2701.

invented, but an essential element of an Article III case or controversy. The majority's notion that a case between friendly parties can be entertained so long as "adversarial presentation of the issues is assured by . . . *amici curiae* [who] defend with vigor" the other side of the issue . . . effects a breathtaking revolution in our Article III jurisprudence.[68]

"There is," said Scalia, quoting Chief Justice John Marshall in *Marbury v. Madison*, "no 'necessity [to] expound and interpret' the law in this case; just a desire to place this Court at the center of the Nation's life."[69] The Court's opinion, said Scalia, "envisions a Supreme Court standing (or rather enthroned) at the apex of government, empowered to decide all constitutional questions, always and everywhere 'primary' in its role."[70]

In its disregard of the constitutional limits on its jurisdiction, the decision is lawless, a judicial coup, bringing to mind Judge Learned Hand's comment: "For myself it would be most irksome to be ruled by a bevy of Platonic Guardians, even if I knew how to choose them, which I assuredly do not."[71]

The Ruling on the Constitutionality of Section 3

The Court went on to hold Section 3 of DOMA unconstitutional as a violation of the equal protection of the law protected by the Fifth Amendment's guarantee of due process of law. Section 3, the Court said, "imposes a disability on [a class of persons] by refusing to acknowledge a status the State finds to be dignified and proper. DOMA instructs . . . all persons with whom same-sex couples interact, including their own children, that their marriage is less worthy than the marriages of others. . . . [N]o legitimate purpose overcomes the purpose and effect to disparage and to injure

68 *Ibid.*, 2702.
69 *Ibid.*, 2703.
70 *Ibid.*, 2698.
71 Learned Hand, *The Bill of Rights* (1958), 73.

those whom the State . . . sought to protect in personhood and dignity."[72]

"'It is a familiar principle of constitutional law,' said Scalia, "'that this Court will not strike down an otherwise constitutional statute on the basis of an alleged illicit legislative motive.' (citation omitted) Or at least it *was* a familiar principle. . . . [T]he majority has declared open season on any law that (in the opinion of the law's opponents and any panel of like-minded federal judges) can be characterized as mean-spirited."[73]

Scalia correctly accused the majority of "affirmatively concealing from the reader the arguments . . . in justification" of Section 3.[74] "Imagine," Scalia said, "a pair of women who marry in Albany and then move to Alabama which does not [recognize same-sex marriage]. When the couple files their next federal tax return, may it be a joint one? Which State's law controls, for federal-law purposes: their State of celebration (which recognizes the marriage) or their State of domicile (which does not)? (Does the answer depend on whether they were just visiting in Albany?) . . . And what about States where the status of an out-of-state same-sex marriage is an unsettled question under local law? . . . DOMA avoided all of this uncertainty by specifying which marriages would be recognized for federal purposes. That is a classic purpose for a definitional provision."[75]

Instead of examining the legal justifications for DOMA, the Court, said Scalia, accuses "the Congress that enacted this law and the President [Clinton] who signed it of . . . [acting] with *malice*—with the *'purpose'* . . . 'to disparage and to injure' same-sex couples. It says that the motivation for DOMA was to 'demean,' . . . ; to 'impose inequality,' . . . ; to 'impose . . . a stigma,' . . . ; to deny people 'equal dignity,' . . . ; to brand gay people as 'unworthy,' . . . ; and to '*humiliat[e]*' their children (emphasis added) . . . All that . . . for supporting an Act that did no more than codify an

72 133 S. Ct. at 2695–96.
73 *Ibid.*, 2707.
74 *Ibid.*, 2708.
75 *Ibid.*

aspect of marriage that had been unquestioned in . . . virtually all societies for virtually all of human history. It is one thing for a society to elect change; it is another for a court of law to impose change by adjudging those who oppose it *hostes humani generis*, enemies of the human race."[76] More Scalia:

> It takes real cheek for today's majority to assure us, as it is going out the door, that a constitutional require-ment to give formal recognition to same-sex marriage is not at issue here—when what has preceded that assur-ance is a lecture on how superior the majority's moral judgment in favor of same-sex marriage is to the Congress's hateful moral judgment against it. I promise you this: The only thing that will "confine" the Court's holding is its sense of what it can get away with. . . .
>
> [The] view that *this* Court will take of state prohibition of same-sex marriage is indicated beyond mistaking by today's opinion. . . . [T]he . . . rationale of today's opin-ion . . . is that DOMA is motivated by "'bare . . . desire to harm'" couples in same-sex marriages. . . . [H]ow inevitable, to reach the same conclusion with regard to state laws denying same-sex couples marital status. . . . [N]o one should be fooled; it is just a matter of listen-ing and waiting for the other shoe.
>
> By . . . declaring anyone opposed to same-sex marriage an enemy of human decency, the majority arms well every challenger to a state law restricting marriage to its traditional definition. . . . [T]hose challengers will lead with this Court's declaration that there is "no legitimate purpose" served by such a law, and will claim that the traditional definition has "the purpose and effect to dis-parage and to injure" the "personhood and dignity" of same-sex couples."[77]

76 *Ibid.*, 2708–09
77 *Ibid.*, 2709–10.

What is Really Wrong with This Decision?

Marriage is a given. It antedates the State. Its nature was established by God himself in *Genesis*.[78] The role of the State with respect to marriage is limited. Human law exists to promote the common good, which is "the sum total of social conditions which allow people, either as groups or as individuals, to reach their fulfillment more fully and more easily."[79] Human law, however, is limited. It does not prescribe every virtue or forbid every vice lest by its unenforceability the law be "despised" and "greater evils" result.[80]

The State should promote marriage (which means one man and one woman) and the family founded on marriage because they are essential to the common good. In the United States, the promotion and regulation of marriage, including its definition as embodied in the law, is a matter for the State governments. That general priority of the State governments in marriage and domestic relations was recognized in all the opinions in *U.S. v. Windsor*. The federal government has no direct power to define or regulate marriage as such. But it does have power to define what the terms "marriage," "spouse," etc., mean when they are used in federal law such as the estate tax. Any such federal definitions, as both sides recognize in *Windsor*, are subject to constitutional limitations such as the Fifth Amendment.

Justice Scalia spelled out some of the practical reasons why Section 3 is reasonable and constitutional.[81] Without addressing those practical justifications, the majority condemned Section 3 as "mean spirited," etc. Equal protection of the law is guaranteed explicitly by the Fourteenth Amendment (which binds only the States) and implicitly by the Fifth Amendment (which binds both the State and federal governments). The Court's invocation of equal protection indicates that, as soon as a new case or

78 *Gen.* 1:27; 2:18–25.
79 CCC, no. 1906.
80 *ST* I, II, Q. 96, art. 2.
81 133 S. Ct. 2707–08.

pseudo-case is presented to it, the Court will strike down State laws defining marriage as the union of one man and one woman. Such a ruling would be an unjust law,[82] not merely because of its violation of constitutional principles but especially because it is beyond the authority of any human lawgiver to reject the mandate of God creating and defining marriage. Such a decree would also precipitate legal compulsion of the Catholic Church to conform to the new definition. The Church cannot so yield. The result will be a thorough—and potentially bloody—persecution of the Church.

How have we come to the point where "one nation under God" can regard an affirmation of the *Genesis* view of marriage as a "mean-spirited" violation of the Constitution? Ideas do have consequences. One reason we are at that point is that our culture and our law have established, in effect, a Dictatorship of Relativism.[83]

82 See Chapter 2.
83 See Chapters 5–8.

PART II. UNDERLYING CAUSES OF PERSECUTION

Introduction

Over half a century ago, while I was still a child, I recall hearing a number of older people offer the following explanation for the great disasters that had befallen Russia: "Men have forgotten God: that's why all this has happened." . . .

And if I were called upon to identify the principal trait of the entire twentieth century, . . . I would repeat once again: *Men have forgotten God.— Aleksandr Solzhenitsyn.*[1]

1   Aleksandr Solzhenitsyn, Templeton Address, May 10, 1983; see *Immaculata*, Sept. 1983, p. 6.

5. THE DICTATORSHIP OF RELATIVISM

"[R]elativism . . . allowing oneself to be carried along with every wind of 'doctrine,'" said Cardinal Ratzinger in his homily at the Mass before he was elected Pope, "seems to be the only attitude that is fashionable. A dictatorship of relativism is being constituted that recognizes nothing as absolute and . . . only leaves the 'I' and its whims as the ultimate measure."[2]

In the Dictatorship of Relativism, nothing is safe from redefinition. The Vatican Mission to the UN described in 2012 the fate of the term, "gender":

> The traditional meaning of gender refers to the grammatical categories of "masculine," "feminine," and "neuter". . . . But . . . the western postmodern *intelligentsia* have developed a very different meaning since the mid-1950s. Feeding both on radical feminism and the homosexual movement . . . they distinguished gender from sex, restricting sex to the biological and physiological characteristics that define men and women, and using gender in reference to what they considered to be the socially constructed roles that a given society would consider proper for men and women. In practice they treated motherhood, the family as founded on marriage between a man and a woman, male and female complementarity, the spousal identity of the human person, femininity and masculinity, heterosexuality as social constructions or stereotypes that would be contrary to equality, discriminatory, and therefore to be culturally deconstructed. At the end of this revolutionary

---

2   Cardinal Joseph Ratzinger, homily at Mass before the conclave that elected him as Pope Benedict XVI.

process, the male and female body itself was viewed as socially constructed.[3]

Laws forbidding discrimination on grounds of "gender identity" or "sexual orientation" tend to define those characteristics not by nature but as decided by that person or the perceptions of others, from time to time and subject to change.[4] Thus a person can decide for himself or herself, with legal effect and from day to day or hour to hour, whether he or she is a man, a woman or both.

Faith, Reason, and Truth

One might wonder how we got to the point, in law and culture, where the desire of a cross-dressing male to use a women's restroom creates a civil rights issue.[5] The answer is pretty simple. But it requires us to go back a few years.

We are living in what Fr. Francis Canavan, S.J., called "the fag end of the Enlightenment," the collapse of the effort by philosophers and politicians, over the past three centuries and more, to build a society as if God did not exist.[6]

The issue is epistemological. "The fundamental dogma of the Enlightenment," wrote Cardinal Ratzinger, now Emeritus Pope Benedict XVI, "is that man must overcome the prejudices inherited from tradition; he must . . . free himself from every authority in order to think on his own, using nothing but his own reason. . . . Truth is no longer an objective datum, apparent to . . . everyone. . . . It . . . [is] something merely external, which each one grasps from his own point of view. . . . The same truth about the good becomes unattainable. . . . The only reference point for each person is what he can conceive on his own as good.

3 Permanent Observer Mission of the Holy See to the UN, Intervention, March 9, 2012; *L'Osservatore Romano* (English), May 23, 2012, p. 6.
4 See, for example, the South Bend, IN, ordinance adopted in 2012. Today's Catholic, April 8, 2012, p. 12.
5 See, for example, Liberty Counsel release, April 23, 2012; www.LCAction.org.
6 *Catholic Eye*, Dec. 10, 1987, 2.

[F]reedom is no longer . . . striving for the good which reason uncovers with help from the community and tradition, but is rather . . . an emancipation from all conditions which prevent each one from following his own reason."[7]

In his first encyclical, which completed Benedict XVI's "first draft of an encyclical on faith,"[8] Pope Francis spoke of the "bond between faith and truth."[9] "In contemporary culture," he said, "we . . . tend to consider the only real truth to be that of technology: . . . . [T]ruth is what works and makes life easier and more comfortable. Nowadays that appears as the only truth that is certain, . . . that can serve as a basis for discussion. . . . Yet . . . we . . . allow for subjective truths of the individual, which consist in fidelity to his or her . . . convictions, yet these are truths valid only for that individual. . . . Truth itself . . . which would . . . explain our life as individuals and in society, is regarded with suspicion. . . . [T]his kind of truth—we hear it said—is what was claimed by . . . the totalitarian movements of the last century, a truth that imposed its own world view . . . to crush the . . . lives of individuals. . . . [W]hat we are left with is relativism, in which the question of universal truth—and . . . the question of God—is no longer relevant. It would be logical from this point of view . . . to sever the bond between religion and truth because it seems to lie at the root of fanaticism, which proves oppressive for anyone who does not share the same beliefs."[10]

The Dictatorship of Relativism is built on three false premises:

<u>Secularism.</u> In 2001, thirteen days after 9/11, Pope John Paul II, in Kazakhstan, warned the leaders of that Islamic republic against a "slavish conformity" to Western culture which is in a "deepening human, spiritual and moral impoverishment" caused

---

7   Cardinal Joseph Ratzinger, *Address to the Consistory of College of Cardinals*, April 3, 1991; see discussion in Charles E. Rice, *What Happened to Notre Dame?* (2009), 103–04.

8   Pope Francis, *Lumen Fidei* (2013), no. 7.

9   *Ibid.*, no. 25.

10 *Ibid.*

by "the fatal attempt to secure the good of humanity by eliminating God, the Supreme Good."[11] Here again, the key is epistemology. In his Regensburg University address, in 2006, Pope Benedict XVI criticized "the self-imposed limitation of reason to the empirically verifiable." That limitation underlies the "dictatorship of relativism." If reason is so limited, "the questions raised by religion and ethics . . . have no place within the purview of collective reason as defined by 'science,' . . . and must be relegated to the realm of the subjective."[12]

In the Dictatorship of Relativism, affirmations of God or of objective morality are considered non-rational and are, therefore, excluded from the public discourse.[13] Is reason, however, incapable of knowing even whether God exists? "[T]his proposition, *God exists*, of itself is self-evident . . . because God is his own existence. . . . Now because we do not know the essence of God, the proposition is not self-evident to us, but needs to be demonstrated by things that are more known to us."[14] We know from reason that an eternal being with no beginning, i.e., God, had to have always existed. The alternative is that there was a time when there was absolutely nothing. But that makes no sense. If there was ever a time when there was nothing, there could never be anything. As Aquinas said, "if at one time nothing was in existence, it would have been impossible for anything to have begun to exist; and thus even now nothing would be in existence—which is absurd."[15] Julie Andrews got it right in *The Sound of Music*: "Nothing comes from nothing. Nothing ever could." It is unreasonable *not* to believe in God.

The only basis for inalienable rights against the State is the creation of the immortal person in the image and likeness of God. Every State that has ever existed, or ever will exist, has gone out

---

11 Pope John Paul II, Address to Cultural Leaders, Astana, Kazakhstan, Sept. 24, 2001.

12 Pope Benedict XVI, University of Regensburg Address, Sept. 12, 2006.

13 William Smith, "The First Amendment and Progress," *Humanitas*, Summer 1987, p. 1.

14 St. Thomas Aquinas, *ST*, I, Q. 2, art. 1.

15 *ST*, I, Q. 2, art. 3.

of business or will go out of business. Every human being that has ever been conceived will live forever. That is why you have transcendent rights against the State. The person does not exist for the State. The State exists for the person. And for the family. But if there is no God, everything is up for grabs. A relativistic secularism is the *de facto* official religion of the United States.[16]

Relativism. The statement that all things are relative is absurd. If it were true, that statement itself would have to be relative. Our universities are full of professors who are sure that they can't be sure of anything. Or if they are not sure even of that, they are sure at least that they are not sure of it. Or they might say that the only propositions that are meaningful are those that can be empirically verified by the scientific method. But that proposition itself cannot be empirically verified.[17] In reality, we can know objective truth, including moral truth, through reason as well as faith.[18]

It goes back again to "the self-limitation of reason to the empirically verifiable."[19] Because relativism denies a knowable, objective moral law, the jurisprudence of relativism is some form of legal positivism, which asserts that there is no knowable higher law that limits what human law can do. A law of any content is valid if it is enacted pursuant to prescribed procedures and is effective. Hans Kelsen, the leading legal positivist of the twentieth century, espoused "philosophical relativism." He said that Auschwitz and the Soviet Gulags were valid law. He could not criticize them as unjust because justice, he said, is "an irrational ideal."[20] Kelsen claimed that relativism is the philosophy of democracy. John Paul responded that relativism leads instead to totalitarianism:

16 See discussion in Sarah Nirenberg, *The Resurgence of Secularism: Hostility Towards Religion in the United States and France*, 5 Wash. U. Jur. Rev. 131 (2012).
17 See Charles E. Rice, *50 Questions on the Natural Law* (1999), 133–34.
18 See generally, Pope John Paul II, *Fides et Ratio* (Faith and Reason) (1998).
19 Pope Benedict XVI, *Address*, September 12, 2006.
20 Hans Kelsen, "The Pure Theory of Law, Part I," 50 *Law Quart. Rev.* 474, 482 (1934).

Only God, the Supreme Good, constitutes the unshakable foundation . . . of morality . . . The Supreme Good and moral good meet in truth: the truth of God . . . and the truth of man, created and redeemed by him. . . . "Totalitarianism arises out of a denial of truth in the objective sense. . . . If one does not acknowledge transcendent truth, then the force of power takes over, and each person tends to . . . impose his own interests or his own opinion, with no regard for the rights of others. . . . "[21]

For most of the past century, the American Ruling Class[22] has pursued what is accurately called "the deliberate dumbing down of America."[23] There should be no surprise at Allan Bloom's statement that for American university students, "the relativity of truth is not a theoretical insight but a moral postulate, the condition of a free society. . . . Relativism is necessary to openness; and this is . . . the only virtue, which all primary education for more than fifty years has dedicated itself to inculcating. Openness–and the relativism that makes it the only plausible stance in the face of various claims to truth . . . is the great insight of our times. The true believer is the real danger."[24] "One cannot escape the fact," said John Paul II in 2002, "that more than in any other historical period, there is a breakdown in the process of handing on moral and religious values between generations."[25] Such a breakdown produces a citizenry ignorant of knowable, moral limits on their own conduct and that of the State. Boobus Americanus tends to be absorbed in pop culture, and to be tolerant of religious persecution (of others) and of other aspects of totalitarianism.

Individualism. The Enlightenment looks on the human person, not as *social* by nature, but as an isolated individual who is merely *sociable* in that he can be made social by his consent. Social

21 Pope John Paul II, *VS*, no. 99, quoting Pope John Paul II, *CA* (1991).
22 See Angelo Codevilla, *The Ruling Class* (2010).
23 Charlotte Thomson Iserbyt, "The Deliberate Dumbing Down of America" (1999).
24 Allan Bloom, *The Closing of the American Mind* (1987), 25–26.
25 Pope John Paul II, *Address*, March 16, 2002.

contract theorists denied the social nature of man. They postulated a state of nature in which each person was an autonomous, isolated individual with no relation to others unless he consents.[26] That is the origin of pro-choice as we know it today. Planned Parenthood didn't think it up. The mother has no relation to her unborn child unless she consents. The husband and wife have no continuing relation unless they continue to consent. And so on. The autonomous individual is the creator of his own morality, i.e., he is his own god. As John Paul II put it, "the roots of the contradiction between the solemn affirmation of human rights and their tragic denial in practice lies in a *notion of freedom* which exalts the isolated individual in an absolute way, and gives no place to solidarity, to openness to others and service of them. . . . If the promotion of the self is understood in terms of absolute autonomy, people inevitably reach the point of rejecting one another. Everyone else is considered an enemy from whom one has to defend oneself. Thus society becomes a mass of individuals placed side by side, but without any mutual bonds. Each one wishes to assert himself independently of the other and in fact intends to make his own interests prevail."[27]

Whatever the autonomous individual chooses is, for him, the right thing to do. That is portrayed as the way to freedom. But authentic freedom cannot be separated from the truth. You are "free" to choose to put sand in the gas tank of your car. But you will no longer be free to drive your car because you have violated the truth of the nature of your car. You are "free" to choose to lie, to fornicate, etc., but you will diminish yourself because you have violated the truth of your nature. You have chosen the moral equivalent of putting sand in your gas tank. And there is one thing the autonomous individual of liberal mythology can never do. He can never put himself out of existence. He is going to live forever and will spend eternity someplace. Where, is up to him.

The liberal mythology of the autonomous individual leads to

26　See Heinrich A. Rommen, *The Natural Law* (Liberty Fund, 1998), ch. 4.
27　*EV*, nos. 19–20.

the dismissal of the family and other associations standing between the individual and the State. As a person with an eternal destiny, man cannot find his fulfillment in the State. The principle of subsidiarity denies the claim of the State to total competence:

> Just as it is wrong to withdraw from the individual and commit to the community at large what private enterprise . . . can accomplish, so too, it is an injustice . . . for a larger and higher organization to arrogate to itself functions which can be performed efficiently by smaller and lower bodies. This . . . fundamental principle of social philosophy . . . retains its full truth today. . . . The true aim of all social activity should be to help individual members of the social body, but never to destroy or absorb them.[28]

"Subsidiarity," said Benedict XVI, "is the most effective antidote against any form of all-encompassing welfare state."[29] The architects of American culture, instead, are the intellectual heirs of Jean Jacques Rousseau (1712–1778), the proponent of both individualism and the total State. Rousseau subordinated the individual to the general will as defined by the State: "When first he opens his eyes, an infant ought to see the fatherland, and up to the day of his death he ought never to see anything else. Every true republican . . . sees nothing but the fatherland, he lives for it alone. . . . "[30] "And when the prince says to him: 'It is expedient for the State that you should die,'" Rousseau's conclusion is that "he ought to die . . . because his life is no longer a mere bounty of nature, but a gift made conditionally by the State."[31]

28 *C in V*, no. 52.
29 *Ibid.*, no. 57.
30 Jean Jacques Rousseau, *Considerations on the Government of Poland* (1772), chap. IV; www.constitution.org/jjr/poland.htm.
31 Jean Jacques Rousseau, *The Social Contract, Book II*, Chapter V; see Clarence Morris, ed., *The Great Legal Philosophers* (1959), 223.

In truth, the "identity" of the human person is that he is "a spiritual and bodily being in relationship with God, with his neighbor and with the material world."[32] "[E]very man is his 'brother's keeper,' because God entrusts us to one another. . . . [I]n view of this entrusting . . . God gives everyone . . . a freedom which possesses an *inherently relational dimension*."[33] Thus, "the full meaning of freedom [is] the gift of self in *service to God and one's brethren*."[34] Our model is the "*Crucified Christ* [who] *reveals the authentic meaning of freedom; he lives it fully in the total gift of himself* and calls his disciples to share in his freedom."[35] As John Paul described it, "the deepest and most authentic meaning of life [is] that of being *a gift which is fully realized in the giving of self*."[36] This truth is "unrecognized because of a . . . consumerist and utilitarian view of life," said Benedict XVI in his third encyclical.[37] "The human being," he said, "is made for gift, which expresses and makes present his transcendent dimension."[38]

An "individualistic concept of freedom ends up by becoming the freedom of 'the strong' against the weak who have no choice but to submit."[39] And the State is stronger than the isolated individual who has turned from God. He cannot defend his rights of conscience because he does not even know what his conscience is or why he has one.

32 *VS*, no. 13.
33 *Ibid.*
34 *VS*, no. 87.
35 *Ibid.*, no. 85.
36 *EV*, no. 49.
37 *C in V*, no. 34.
38 *Ibid.*
39 *EV*, no. 19.

6. CONSCIENCE REDEFINED

Conscience is a judgment of reason whereby the human person recognizes the moral quality of a concrete act that he is going to perform, is . . . performing . . . or has . . . completed.—*Catechism of the Catholic Church*[40]

How Does Conscience Work?

One of the first casualties of the limitation of reason to empirical or scientific knowledge is a sound understanding of conscience. "[C]onscience expresses itself in acts of 'judgment' which reflect the truth about the good and not in arbitrary decisions."[41] "The judgment of conscience is a *practical judgment*, which makes known what man must do or not do, or which assesses an act already performed by him. It . . . applies to a concrete situation the rational conviction that one must love and do good and avoid evil."[42]

Our judgment of conscience, however, may be wrong. Whether we are culpable for that error will depend on whether we have fulfilled three duties to conscience:

1. Form that judgment, just as you would form any other judgment, such as what car to buy, etc. The first duty, in forming that judgment, is to consult the directions given to us by God through the natural law, the Ten Commandments (which are specifications of the natural law) and the teachings of the Church.
2. Follow the judgment of your conscience if it is clear and certain. This is your duty even if that judgment turns out to be

40 CCC, no. 1778.
41 VS, no. 61.
42 VS, no. 59.

wrong. If your judgment is objectively wrong, you may be culpable for failing to form it properly.

3. If in doubt, try to resolve the doubt. If the doubt persists, for example, as to whether it is right to take for yourself that pen that seems to be forgotten, or abandoned, on the desk, don't take it. If you do take it, you will be choosing to do what, for all you know, is wrong. Instead, take the safer course. Don't take the pen.[43]

In the real world, as St. Thomas tells us: "If . . . we consider one act in the moral order, it is impossible for it to be morally both good and evil."[44] "Moral truth is objective," said John Paul II at the 1993 World Youth Day in Denver, "and a properly formed conscience can perceive it."[45]

Conscience and God

As John Paul II put it: "Conscience is *the witness of God himself*, whose voice and judgment penetrate the depth of man's soul, calling him . . . strongly yet gently to obedience."[46] Cardinal Newman made the striking point that conscience proves the very existence of a "Supernatural and Divine" being "to whom our love and veneration look":

> If, as is the case, we feel responsibility, are ashamed, are frightened, at transgressing the voice of conscience, this implies that there is One to whom we are responsible, before whom we are ashamed, whose claims upon us we fear. If, on doing wrong, we feel the same . . . sorrow which overwhelms us in hurting a mother; if, on doing right, we enjoy the same sunny serenity of mind, the same . . . delight which follows on our receiving praise from a father, we certainly have within us the image of

43 CCC, no. 1776–1802.
44 *ST*, I, II, Q. 20, art. 6.
45 N.Y. Times, Aug. 15, 1993.
46 VS, no. 64.

some person, to whom our love and veneration look, in whose smile we find our happiness . . . towards whom we direct our pleadings, in whose anger we are troubled. . . . These feelings . . . require for their . . . cause an intelligent Being; we are not affectionate towards a stone, nor do we feel shame before a horse or a dog; we have no remorse or compunction on breaking mere human law; yet . . . conscience excites all these painful emotions, confusion, foreboding, self-condemnation; and on the other hand it sheds upon us a deep peace, a sense of security, a resignation and a hope, which there is no sensible, no earthly object to elicit, "The wicked flees when no one pursueth;" then why does he flee? whence his terror? Who is it that he sees in solitude, in darkness, in the hidden chambers of his heart? If the cause of these emotions does not belong to this visible world, the Object to which his perception is directed must be Supernatural and Divine; and thus the phenomena of Conscience . . . impress the imagination with the picture of a Supreme Governor, a Judge, holy, just, powerful, all-seeing, retributive, and is the creative principle of religion, as the Moral Sense is the principle of ethics.[47]

Conscience and the Pope

Certainly, if I am obliged to bring religion into after-dinner toasts (which indeed does not seem quite the thing) I shall drink—to the Pope, if you please, — still, to conscience first and to the Pope afterwards.— Cardinal John Henry Newman, *Letter to the Duke of Norfolk*[48]

---

47 John Henry Cardinal Newman, *Grammar of Assent*, ch. 5, sec. 1 (Garden City, N.Y.: Doubleday, 1955), 101.
48 See discussion in Charles E. Rice, *What Happened to Notre Dame?* (2009), 110 et seq.

You might be surprised to know that Cardinal Joseph Ratzinger, who later became Benedict XVI, agreed with Newman. "[T]he toast to conscience indeed must precede the toast to the pope," said Ratzinger to the United States bishops in 1991, "because without conscience there would not be a papacy."[49]

"The pope," said Ratzinger, "cannot impose commandments on . . . Catholics because he . . . finds it expedient. Such a modern, voluntaristic concept of authority can only distort the . . . meaning of the papacy. . . . The . . . teaching authority of the pope consists of his being the advocate of the Christian memory. The pope does not impose from without. Rather he elucidates the Christian memory and defends it. For this reason the toast to conscience indeed must precede the toast to the pope because without conscience there would not be a papacy. All power that the papacy has is power of conscience."[50]

Everyone has a pope, a visible authority on moral questions. If it is not the real pope, it will be a pope of the individual's own choosing—whether Rush Limbaugh, Barack Obama, or the individual himself. It makes sense that we have one pope instead of 7 billion, which would involve the natural law and its Lawgiver in a chaos of contradictions. "Christians have a great help for the formation of conscience *in the Church and her Magisterium*," said John Paul II. "In forming their consciences," John Paul continued, "the Christian faithful must give careful attention to the . . . teaching of the Church. For the Catholic Church is by the will of Christ the teacher of truth. Her charge is to . . . teach . . . that truth which is Christ, and . . . to declare . . . the principles of the moral order which derive from human nature itself. . . . The Church puts herself . . . at the service of conscience, helping it to avoid being tossed to and fro by every wind of doctrine proposed by human deceit . . . and helping it . . . to attain the truth with certainty."[51]

---

49 *Ibid.*; Cardinal Joseph Ratzinger, *Conscience and Truth*, 10th workshop for bishops, February 1991, Dallas, Texas.

50 *Ibid.*

51 Pope John Paul II, *VS* (1993), no. 64, quoting Vatican II, *Dignitatis Humanae*, no. 14.

Conscience and the State

Conscience is entitled to protection by the State because conscience is more than a merely human judgment. It is "the sacred place where God speaks to man."[52] Speaking of legalized abortion and euthanasia, John Paul II insisted that the law should protect the right of "conscientious objection."[53] This is especially true in any situation where the State compels one to violate, contrary to the judgment of conscience, a prohibitory law of God. "To refuse to take part in committing an injustice is not only a moral duty; it is also a basic human right. . . . [T]he opportunity to refuse to take part in the phases of consultation, preparation and execution of these acts against life should be guaranteed to physicians, healthcare personnel, and directors of hospitals, clinics and convalescent facilities."[54]

The *Catechism* accurately defines conscience as "a judgment of reason."[55] The redefinition of conscience as an act of the will trivializes conscience and plays into the hands of a hostile State. Since the "dictatorship of relativism"[56] denies that reason can know anything beyond "the empirically verifiable,"[57] reason cannot reach objective moral truth. Questions of religion and ethics "must . . . be relegated to the realm of the subjective." Conscience becomes merely a personal decision entirely up to the individual. "The [person] decides, on the basis of his experiences, what he considers tenable in matters of religion, and subjective 'conscience' becomes the sole arbiter of what is ethical."[58] John Paul noted "a tendency to grant to the individual conscience the prerogative of independently determining the criteria of good and evil and then acting accordingly. [In such] an individualistic ethic . . . each individual is faced with his own truth, different from the

52 *VS*, no. 58.
53 *EV*, no. 73.
54 *Ibid.*, nos. 74, 89.
55 CCC, no. 1778.
56 Cardinal Joseph Ratzinger, Homily, April 18, 2005.
57 Pope Benedict XVI, Address, Sept. 12, 2006.
58 *Ibid.*

truth of others. Taken to its extreme consequences, this individualism leads to a denial of the very idea of human nature."[59]

If conscience is merely an act of your will with no relation to objective right and wrong, it becomes merely a choice, essentially an expression of personal, even idiosyncratic, taste no more subject to anyone else's objective moral approval or disapproval than would be your choice of vanilla or chocolate ice cream. If your claim of a right of conscience is grounded on no objective moral criteria, it lacks any coherent basis for any transcendent claim to immunity against oppression by the State.[60] Whether the State will override the entirely subjective decision of your conscience, even as to a prohibitory law of God, becomes a matter of State discretion, a utilitarian and comparatively trivial issue. One reason the Constitution will offer no protection here is that the Supreme Court, following the culture, has distorted the Constitution to require a strict separation of morality from law.

59   *VS*, no. 32.
60   See Pope John Paul II, *VS*, no. 32.

7. THE CONSTITUTION: MORAL NEUTRALITY

> Of all the dispositions and habits which lead to political prosperity, Religion and morality are indispensable supports. . . . And let us with caution indulge the supposition that morality can be maintained without religion. . . . [R]eason and experience both forbid us to expect that National morality can prevail in exclusion of religious principle. — *George Washington, Farewell Address, Sept. 19, 1796.*[61]

The First Amendment and Religion

On September 24–25, 1789, the First Congress proposed to the States the Bill of Rights, including the First Amendment religion clauses which provide: "Congress shall make no law respecting an establishment of religion, or prohibiting the free exercise thereof." (The Supreme Court has held that virtually all the protections of the Bill of Rights, including the religion clauses, are binding upon the States.[62])

On the same days that it approved the First Amendment, the Congress requested the President to "recommend to the people . . . a day of public thanksgiving and prayer . . . acknowledging . . . the many . . . favors of Almighty God, especially by affording them an opportunity peaceably to establish a Constitution."[63] President Washington did so, saying: "it is the duty of all nations to acknowledge the providence of Almighty God, to obey His will,

---

61 W.B. Allen, ed., *George Washington* (1988), 521.
62 See *Abington School District v. Schempp*, 374 U.S. 203, 215 (1963).
63 Annals of Congress, Sept. 25, 1789.

to be grateful for His benefits, and humbly to implore His protection and favor."[64]

The First Amendment barred Congress from establishing a national church or interfering with established churches in the States. It was not intended to prevent the federal government from affirming God as long as it maintained neutrality among religious, or at least Christian, sects. Justice Joseph Story, who served on the Supreme Court from 1811 to 1845, and who was a Unitarian, spelled out the meaning of the religion clauses:

> Probably at the time of the adoption . . . of the first amendment . . . , the general if not the universal sentiment in America was, that Christianity ought to receive encouragement from the state so far as was not incompatible with the private rights of conscience and the freedom of religious worship. An attempt to level all religions, and to make it a matter of state policy to hold all in utter indifference, would have created universal disapprobation. . . .
>
> The real object of the amendment was . . . to exclude all rivalry among Christian sects, and to prevent any national ecclesiastical establishment which should give to a hierarchy the exclusive patronage of the national government.[65]

A Christian Nation?

Over the succeeding decades, a broadly Christian character of American culture and law gained occasional and limited recognition by the Supreme Court. In 1844, the Court upheld the will of Stephen Girard, who bequeathed money to establish a school for

64 President George Washington, Proclamation, Oct. 3, 1789. See text and discussion in Robert L. Cord, *Separation of Church and State* (1982), 51–53.
65 Joseph Story, Commentaries on the Constitution of the United States (1891), Secs. 1874, 1876, 1877.

orphans. His will prohibited ministers of any sect from visiting the school and limited instruction to pure morality to the implicit exclusion of any instruction in religion. "It is also said, and truly," said the Court, "that the Christian religion is a part of the common law of Pennsylvania . . . in this qualified sense, that its divine origin and truth are admitted, and therefore it is not to be maliciously and openly reviled and blasphemed against, to the annoyance of believers or the injury of the public." The Court upheld the will, saying that for it to fail, it must expressly demonstrate "not only that Christianity is not to be taught; but that it is to be impugned or repudiated."[66]

In *Church of the Holy Trinity v. U.S.*,[67] the Supreme Court held that a federal statute prohibiting the immigration of persons under contract to perform labor, did not apply to an English minister who entered this country under contract to preach at a New York church. The Court said: "[N]o purpose . . . against religion can be imputed to any legislation . . . because this is a religious people." After quoting historical documents, the Court continued:

> These, and many other matters . . . add . . . to the mass of organic utterances that this is a Christian nation. In the face of all these, shall it be believed that . . . Congress . . . intended to make it a misdemeanor for a church . . . to contract for the services of a Christian minister residing in another nation?[68]

Despite such early affirmations by courts of the role of Christianity,[69] demographic changes brought a new consensus. As Justice William Brennan noted in 1963, "our religious composition makes us a vastly more diverse people than were our forefathers. They knew differences chiefly among Protestant sects. Today the Nation is far more heterogeneous religiously, including

66 *Vidal v. Girard's Executors*, 43 U.S. 126, 198 (1844).
67 143 U.S. 457 (1892).
68 *Id.* at 470–71.
69 See also *People v. Ruggles*, 8 Johns. (N.Y.) 290, 293 (1811); *Pirkey Bros. v. Commonwealth*, 114 S. E. 764, 765 (VA, 1922).

. . . minorities not only of Catholics and Jews but as well of those who worship according to no version of the Bible and those who worship no God at all."[70]

Religious Neutrality

Reflecting—as well as influencing—cultural changes, the Supreme Court has interpreted the Establishment Clause to require governmental neutrality, not among Christian sects as originally intended, but as between the general religions of theism and non-theism. In *Torcaso v. Watkins*,[71] the Court held in 1961 that a Maryland requirement that State employees declare their belief in God unconstitutionally invaded the "freedom of belief and religion" because it puts the State "on the side of one . . . sort of believers—those who are willing to say they believe in 'the existence of God.'"[72] The Court said that, "neither a State nor the Federal Government . . . can constitutionally . . . aid all religions as against non-believers, and neither can aid those religions based on a belief in the existence of God as against those religions founded on different beliefs."[73] In a footnote, the Court said, "Among religions in this country which do not teach what would commonly be considered a belief in the existence of God are Buddhism, Taoism, Ethical Culture, Secular Humanism and others."[74]

In *Abington School District v. Schempp*,[75] the Court, quoting *Torcaso*, adopted this neutrality between theism and non-theism as the mandate of the Establishment Clause.[76] In *Schempp*, the Court denied that its decisions established a "religion of secularism."[77]

---

70 *Abington School District v. Schempp*, 374 U.S. 203, 239–40 (1963).
71 367 U.S. 488, 490, 495 (1961).
72 *Ibid.*, 490.
73 *Ibid.*, 495.
74 *Ibid.*
75 374 U.S. 203 (1963).
76 *Ibid.*, 220.
77 *Ibid.*, 225.

It is fair to conclude, however, that it is practically impossible for government to maintain neutrality on the existence of God without implicitly establishing a religion of agnostic secularism. Suppose a public school teacher is asked whether the four affirmations of God in the Declaration of Independence are true. If he answers "Yes," that is a preference of theism. If he says, "No," that is a preference of atheism. The correct answer, according to the Court's theory, is to suspend judgment and say in effect: "I (speaking as a government official) do not know." But this is a preference of agnosticism, which is itself a religion according to the Court. In his concurring opinion in *Schempp*, Justice Brennan said that the decision did not require the invalidation of "various *patriotic* exercises . . . which, whatever may have been their origins, *no longer have a religious purpose or meaning*. The reference to divinity in the revised pledge of allegiance, for example, may merely recognize the historical fact that our Nation *was believed to have been founded 'under God.'* Thus reciting the pledge may be no more of a religious exercise than the reading aloud of Lincoln's Gettysburg Address, which contains an allusion to the same historical fact."[78]

Moral Neutrality and the Law

"Our Constitution," said President John Adams in 1798, "was made only for a moral and religious people. It is wholly inadequate to the government of any other."[79]

The question here is whether moral judgments of the people can serve as a basis for law. George Washington would have said yes. If, however, the answer is "No," then laws defining marriage as a union of one man and one woman are dead on arrival. As Justice Scalia put it in 1993: "State laws against bigamy, same-sex marriage, adult incest, prostitution, masturbation,

78   *Ibid.*, 303–04 (1963) (emphasis added).
79   See discussion in Charles E. Rice, *The Supreme Court and Public Prayer* (1964), 47.

adultery, fornication, bestiality, and obscenity are . . . sustainable only in light of [the] validation of laws based on moral choices."[80] Indeed, most laws can be traced to some moral foundation.

The Constitution did not attempt to define the relation between morality and the enactment of laws. The subject came up in the Supreme Court as a discussion of natural law in *Calder v. Bull*[81] in 1798. The Court held that the prohibition of ex post facto laws, in Article I, Section 10 of the Constitution, applied only to penal, and not civil, laws. Justice Samuel Chase went on to say that if a state did enact a genuinely ex post facto law, it would be invalid even if it had not been prohibited by the Constitution: "There are . . . principles in our free Republican governments," Chase said, "which will . . . over-rule an apparent and flagrant abuse of legislative power."[82]

Justice James Iredell rejected this natural law approach: If the legislature "pass a law, within . . . their constitutional power, the Court cannot pronounce it to be void, merely because it is, in their judgment, contrary to the principles of natural justice. *The ideas of natural justice are regulated by no fixed standard: the ablest and purest men have differed upon the subject.*"[83]

It was "Chase's views, not Iredell's, that were in the mainstream of late eighteenth-century American jurisprudence."[84] Iredell's view is in line with the Protestant theory that private judgment controls, with "no fixed standard." If Iredell is right, the natural law is relatively useless as a higher standard for law and a guide for human conduct. Even if we recognize that there is a natural law, how do we know what it means? Iredell's view, however, prevailed in American culture and law.

---

80 *Lawrence v. Texas*, 539 U.S. 558, 590 (2003) (Scalia, J., dissenting).
81 *Calder v. Bull*, 3 Dallas 386 (1798).
82 *Ibid.*, 387–89.
83 *Ibid.*, 399 (emphasis added); see discussion in Edward S. Corwin, "Natural Law and Constitutional Law," 3 *Nat. Law Inst. Proceedings*, 47, 59–61 (1950).
84 Stephen B. Presser, *Recapturing the Constitution* (1994), 120–21.

Morality and Laws Defining Marriage

Can morality serve as a justification for law? The Supreme Court now says: No. That answer reflects the establishment of agnostic secularism as the *de facto* official religion of the United States.

In *Lawrence v. Texas*,[85] decided ten years to the day before the *Windsor* case, the Court held unconstitutional a Texas law making consensual "deviate sexual intercourse" a crime. The Court overruled *Bowers v. Hardwick*[86] which had upheld a Georgia law that made such sodomy a crime. In *Bowers*, the Court had upheld morality as a basis for law: "The law is constantly based on notions of morality, and if all laws representing essentially moral choices are to be invalidated . . . the courts will be very busy indeed."[87] In *Lawrence*, however, the Court adopted Justice John Paul Stevens' dissent in *Bowers* in which he said:

> Our prior cases make two propositions . . . clear. First, the fact that the . . . majority in a State has traditionally viewed a . . . practice as immoral is not a sufficient reason for upholding a law prohibiting the practice. . . . Second . . . decisions by married persons, concerning . . . their physical relationship . . . are a form of "liberty" protected by the Due Process Clause of the Fourteenth Amendment. Moreover, this protection extends to intimate choices by unmarried as well as married persons.[88]

In *U.S. v. Windsor*, the Court did not explicitly discuss morality as a justification for law, although it did say, quoting *Lawrence,* that "[p]rivate, consensual sexual intimacy between two adult persons of the same sex may not be punished by the State, and it can form 'but one element in a personal bond that is more enduring.'"[89] In his *Windsor* dissent, Justice Scalia said:

85 539 U.S. 558 (2003).
86 478 U.S. 186 (1986).
87 *Ibid.*, 196.
88 *Ibid.*, 216.
89 131 S. Ct. at 2692, quoting *Lawrence* 539 U.S. at 558, 567.

[T]he Constitution does not forbid the government to enforce traditional moral and sexual norms. . . . I will not swell the U.S. Reports with restatements of that point. It is enough to say that the Constitution neither requires nor forbids our society to approve of same-sex marriage, much as it neither requires nor forbids us to approve of no-fault divorce, polygamy, or the consumption of alcohol.

However, even setting aside traditional moral disapproval of same-sex marriage (or indeed same-sex sex), there are many perfectly valid—indeed, downright boring—justifying rationales for this legislation. Their existence ought to be the end of this case.[90]

Needed: A Moral Interpreter

Want a guaranteed sure thing? Bet that the Supreme Court, barring an unlikely change in its composition or mind-set, will exclude the moral judgment of the people as a justification for State laws defining marriage as the union of one man and one woman. And it will declare such laws invalid. Such a result would astonish the Founders and succeeding generations. We have arrived at this point, however, through a cultural and ultimately legal weakness in the Founding.

Either the government is limited by a knowable higher moral law—the natural law—or it is not. If it is not so limited, it is positivistic.[91] If it is so limited, there must be someone, outside the government and the people, who can provide morally authoritative interpretations of that natural law. The natural law is the law of God and Christ is God. "Christ . . . lives in the Church, and through her teaches, governs and sanctifies."[92] Therefore, the most appropriate moral interpreter of the natural law is the Vicar

90 133 S. Ct. at 2707.
91 See Chapter 5.
92 Pop Paul VI, *Ecclesiam Suam* (1961), nos. 30, 35.

of Christ on earth. The Catholic Church argues "on the basis of reason and natural law" so as "to help form consciences in political life" and to "reawaken the spiritual energy" needed for justice to prevail.[93] This does not mean that the Church should exercise any direct influence on decisions of the courts or other governmental bodies. Rather, what is needed is an external moral interpreter. When the Supreme Court decrees that unborn babies may be killed, objecting citizens ought to be able to point to a source that is accepted by the community as the interpreter of the overriding natural law. Otherwise, we are driven to morality by consensus and thence to legal positivism.[94] If the State is its own interpreter of the natural law, it is not really subject to it at all. And if the State claims to make only legal interpretations, leaving moral questions to the private realm, that in itself is taking a moral position: that law and morality are separated and that the state can act without regard to the moral law. That is what is happening with same-sex "marriage." Nor can the majority provide security as an interpreter of the natural law, for someone must decide what is the consensus, which brings us back to State control.

No charter of government can survive the erosion of the culture that gave it birth. The Founders of the American republic tried to make it Christian without the Church. The system worked for a time because it drew upon the capital inherited from pre-Reformation Catholic Christendom. The failure of the Founders and the founding culture to recognize the moral authority of the Vicar of Christ cut the new republic off from the living Christian tradition and ensured that it would draw no further income from that source. Private judgment was the rule in matters of religion and morality. And it was to be expected that the State would claim the right to exercise its own private judgment as to its own conduct, including its regulation of the conduct of the people.

The point is that no State can long remain subject to the natural moral law unless the people freely recognize, and the State

93   *DCE*, no. 28 (a).
94   See Chapter 5.

acknowledges, that the higher law is from God and that its custody is in the Vicar of Christ. This would be a moral recognition, not a legal establishment. It would reconnect the community with the moral treasury of the Church founded by Christ.

Every society, like every man, has to have a god. There has to be an ultimate authority. If it is not the real God, speaking through the Vicar of Christ (and Christ is God), it will be a god of man's own making. This may be man himself, the consensus, the courts—whatever. Ultimately, in the absence of an external, morally authoritative interpreter, that moral authority will center in the State, which already possesses the coercive power. The conflict, then, is between the claim of the Catholic Church and the claim of the total State. It is not surprising, therefore, that the modern totalitarian State sees the Catholic Church as its main enemy.[95]

---

95 See Charles E. Rice, *Beyond Abortion: The Theory and Practice of the Secular State* (1979), 55–57.

8. THE CONSTITUTION:
STILL TAKEN SERIOUSLY?

The exchange with Speaker [Nancy] Pelosi . . . occurred as follows:

> **CNSNews.com:** "Madam Speaker, where specifically does the Constitution grant Congress the authority to enact an individual health insurance mandate?

> **Pelosi:** "Are you serious? Are you serious?"

> **CNSNews.com:** "Yes, yes I am."

Pelosi then shook her head before taking a question from another reporter.96

Nancy Pelosi has a point. For the Ruling Class today, the concept of the government as having only delegated and limited powers is a prehistoric curiosity. To see how far we have come, let's take a look at that "prehistoric" charter of government that was described by Viscount James Bryce as "the greatest single contribution ever made to Government as an applied science."97

The Basic Structure

Until the United States Constitution, the story of liberty had been one of struggle to curb the otherwise unlimited power of government, as seen in Magna Carta, the Petition of Right in 1628, and the English Bill of Rights of 1689. But, in 1789, the Constitution created a federal system of government, that is, one with divided

---

96 www.cnsnews.com, October 22, 2009.
97 Viscount James Bryce, O.M., *The Study of American History* (1921), 53.

powers. It created a limited government of the United States possessing only the powers delegated to it by the states. That government had implied powers which were limited to the implementation of the delegated powers. Under the division of powers, what has since come to be called "the federal government" was limited to its delegated powers and the states continued to possess all powers inherent in government except as limited by the Constitution. Within the federal government, power was separated among the legislative, executive, and judicial branches, with checks and balances built in to prevent any one or two branches from dominating. The Constitution itself was a bill of rights, since the limitation of government was seen as the most effective safeguard of liberty. In 1791, the ten amendments of the Bill of Rights were added to emphasize the limited character of the new government. The first eight restricted the federal government—and not the states. For protection against their state governments the people relied on their state constitutions and state courts. The last two amendments in the Bill of Rights restated the obvious. The Ninth provided: "The enumeration in the Constitution of certain rights shall not be construed to deny or disparage others retained by the people." And the Tenth stated: "The powers not delegated to the United States by the Constitution, nor prohibited by it to the States, are reserved to the States respectively, or to the people." In 1868, the Fourteenth Amendment forbade any State to "abridge the privileges or immunities of citizens of the United States"; to "deprive any person of life, liberty, or property, without due process of law"; and to "deny to any person within its jurisdiction the equal protection of the laws."[98]

Congressional Empowerment

Back in the day, the question on proposed legislation was: "Where in the Constitution is Congress given the power to do that?" In practice, Congress now can do whatever it wants unless specifically

98 See Charles E. Rice, *The Winning Side* (2000), 38, 47–48.

forbidden by the Constitution as interpreted by Congress itself and the Supreme Court.

The Sixteenth Amendment gave Congress unlimited power to tax incomes, which now includes the power to tax local and personal activities including, as seen in Obamacare, the failure to act as Congress prescribes.[99] Article I, Section 8, of the Constitution gives Congress "Power To Lay and collect Taxes . . . to pay the Debts and provide for the common Defense and general Welfare of the United States." The remaining clauses of Section 8 enumerate the specific powers delegated to Congress: to regulate commerce, declare war, etc. In 1936, the Supreme Court held that the General Welfare power to tax and spend is not limited to the objects specified in the remaining clauses of Section 8.[100] The Court did say that the appropriations must be for the *general* welfare and not for local or special interests, but the Court has left it practically to Congress's discretion as to what purposes are for the "general" welfare. Although the Court does not explicitly give Congress a power to *regulate* for whatever purposes it believes to be for the general welfare, this, too, is an illusion. The power to appropriate carries with it the power to impose regulations to govern the use of the appropriation. "It is hardly lack of due process for the Government to regulate that which it subsidizes."[101] With federal money comes federal control. Always. There is no such thing as a free lunch. This is the basis for subsidy programs, such as Obamacare, under which states and private persons accepting federal money are subject to federal regulation of the way the money is spent.[102]

Judicial Empowerment

The Supreme Court has interpreted the post-Civil War Fourteenth Amendment so as to incorporate and apply to the State virtually all

99 *National Federation of Independent Businesses v. Sebelius*, 132 S. Ct. 2566 (2012).
100 *U.S. v. Butler*, 297 U.S. 1 (1936).
101 *Wickard v. Filburn*, 317 U.S. 111, 131 (1942).
102 See Charles E. Rice, *The Winning Side* (2000), 45–46.

the protections embodied in the Bill of Rights.[103] This Incorporation doctrine has fastened upon the States a uniform obligation to comply with every interpretation by the Court of those provisions of the Bill of Rights, including the Court's invention of unspecified rights—such as the right to reproductive privacy.[104]

The Constitution, by necessary implication, empowers the Supreme Court, and such courts as Congress may create, to interpret the laws.[105] The President and members of Congress are bound by oath to measure their own actions by the Constitution.[106] The Constitution did not specify the extent, if any, to which the Congress and Executive would be bound by Supreme Court interpretations, including holdings that a law is unconstitutional. It was not until 1958 that the Supreme Court asserted that its decisions are the supreme law of the land.[107] Congress and the Executive now habitually defer to Supreme Court decisions as conclusive as to the meaning of a law or its constitutionality. This attitude of deference permeates the culture, as seen in the apparent assumption by public officials and citizens alike that whether the legality of same-sex "marriage" will be mandated is for the Supreme Court to decide, subject only to the adoption of a constitutional amendment to overrule the Court.

Executive Empowerment

In his 2013 State of the Union Address, President Obama urged legislation to deal with climate change. "But if Congress won't act soon to protect future generations," he said, "I will." This is a recurrent Obama theme, not only promising "executive actions" but actually issuing numerous executive orders contrary to, or unauthorized by, enacted law. As in his delaying of enforcement of

103 See *Abington School District v. Schempp*, 374 U.S. 203, 225 (1963), discussed in Chapter 7.
104 *Griswold v. Conn.* 381 U.S. 479, 484 (1965).
105 *Marbury v. Madison*, 5 U.S. 138 (1 Cranch) 138 (1800).
106 Art II, Sec. 1; Art. IV.
107 *Cooper v. Aaron*, 358 U.S. 1 (1958).

the employer mandate in Obamacare, he has refused to enforce laws, not because of any constitutional objection but for policy and political reasons.[108]

The accelerating persecution of religion as seen in the Health Care Mandate and other instances could not have occurred without the President's liberation of his Administration from Constitutional and statutory restraints. Nor could it have occurred if there were any effective Congressional opposition to that liberation. "Republican leaders," as Professor Emeritus Angelo Codevilla of Boston University recently said, "have been partners in the expansion of government, indeed, in the growth of a government-based 'ruling class.' They have relished that role despite their voters. Thus these leaders gradually solidified their choice to no longer represent what had been their constituency, but to openly adopt the identity of junior partners in that ruling class."[109]

An Odd Silence

If you want confirmation that the Ruling Class does not take the Constitution seriously, consider this:

Two questions will be a source of astonishment to future

---

108 See "Obama: If Congress won't act, I will," *Newsday*, Oct. 31, 2011; Heritage Foundation, "Five Ways Obama is Circumventing the Legislative Branch," morningbell@heritage.org, June 29, 2011; Brett Talley, "Dispensing with the Constitution: Obama's Executive Caprice," *Weekly Standard*, Jan. 14, 2003; Sen. Ted Cruz (R-TX), "The Legal Limit: The Obama Administration's Attempts to Expand Federal Power," April 9, 2013, press@cruz.senate.gov. John N. Hall, "Presidential Lawlessness: It's So Cool," *American Thinker*, Aug. 19, 2013; Kevin D. Williamson, "The Front Man: Face of the Lawless Bureaucracy," *National Review Online*, Aug. 5, 2013; Charles Krauthammer, "Can President Obama Write His Own Laws?," *So. Bend Tribune*, Aug. 18, 2013. See generally, Aaron Klein and Brenda J. Elliott, *Impeachable Offenses: The Case for Removing Barack Obama from Office* (2013).

109 Angelo Codevilla, "As Country Club Republicans Link Up With the Democratic Ruling Class, Millions of Voters are Orphaned," www.forbes.com, Feb. 20, 2013.

historians: <u>First</u>: How was Barack Obama twice elected President without making the customary full disclosure of his personal and academic background and without the usual scrutiny of that background by the media or anyone else? <u>Second</u>, why had no leader, or vocal member, of either party in Congress ever suggested a Congressional inquiry into the threshold question of the President's eligibility for that office?

The eligibility controversy involves significant issues of fact and law that deserve some sort of official resolution. I offer no conclusion as to whether President Obama is eligible for his office or not. But the citizens whom the pundits deride as "birthers" have raised legitimate questions.[110] That legitimacy is fueled by Obama's curious, even bizarre refusal to consent to the release of relevant records.[111] Perhaps there is nothing to the issues raised. Or perhaps there is. This is potentially serious business. If it turns out that Obama knew he was ineligible when he campaigned and when he took the oath as President, it would be the biggest political fraud in the history of the world. As long as Obama refuses to make full disclosure, speculation will grow and grow, into the future, without any necessary relation to the truth. The first step toward resolving the issue is full discovery and disclosure of the facts. The courts are not the only entities empowered to deal with such a question. The Twelfth Amendment gives the House of Representatives a contingent but potentially decisive role in the election of a President. The House is, therefore, an appropriate body to inquire into the facts and legal implications of a President's disputed eligibility. A committee of the House should be authorized to conduct an investigation into the eligibility issue. "The American people do not know whether the current President achieved election by misrepresenting, innocently or by fraud, his eligibility for that office. . . . It would be a public service for the House of Representatives . . . to determine those facts

---

110 See Jerome R. Corsi, *Where's the Birth Certificate? The Case that Barack Obama is not Eligible to be President* (2011).

111 See Angelo Codevilla, "The Chosen One," *Claremont Review of Books*, Summer 2011.

and to recommend any indicated changes in the law or the Constitution."[112]

The lack of Congressional interest in determining the facts on eligibility is perhaps the most striking evidence that the Constitution is only selectively, at best, accepted by the Ruling Class as a restraint on its discretion. If you think Congress will enthusiastically respond to invocations of constitutional text to prevent religious persecution or any other abuse—think again. If Congress shows no interest at all in the threshold issue of presidential eligibility, what makes you think any other language of the Constitution will stop a persecution?

A Religious Conflict

On November 13, 2008, Cardinal James Francis Stafford, in an address to the John Paul II Institute in Washington, D.C., spoke of his efforts "to strengthen the Catholic faithful, as St. John did in the Book of the Apocalypse, against the ever increasing pretensions of the state making itself absolute." He said:

> On November 4, 2008 a cultural earthquake hit America. Senator[s] . . . Obama and . . . Biden were elected President and Vice President . . . with a significant majority of their Party in . . . Congress supporting their deadly vision of human life. . . . [I]f their proposals should be . . . enacted, it would be impossible for the American bishops to repeat in the future what their predecessors described the United States in 1884 as "this home of freedom."[113]

If taken seriously, the Constitution could provide a legal barrier to the enactment of such an anti-life agenda. But the Constitution will not alone offer a barrier to that agenda and

112 Charles E. Rice, "Obama's Eligibility: A New Approach", charlesrice.blog-townhall.com, Feb. 7, 2011 (this essay was sent in February, 2011, to the Republican leaders, and other members, of the House of Representatives).
113 John L. Allen, Jr., Daily Blog, Nov. 21, 2008.

persecution because the conflict transcends the legal and the constitutional. It is, at root, a religious conflict. In his definitive book, "The Ruling Class," Professor Angelo Codevilla precisely identified the ideology of America's Ruling Class as itself a religion:

> Its principal article of faith, its claim to the right to decide for others, is precisely that it knows things scientifically, and operates by standards beyond others' comprehension. They claim moral authority as priests of what they claim are ultimate truths.
>
> While the unenlightened believe that man is created in the image and likeness of God, and that we are subject to His and His nature's laws, the enlightened ones *know* that we are products of evolution, driven by chance, the environment, and the will to primacy. . . .
>
> Consensus among the right people is the only standard of truth. Facts and logic matter only insofar as proper authority acknowledges them.[114]

Professor Codevilla stressed the need to challenge the premises of that secular religion: "Because aggressive, intolerant secularism is the moral and intellectual basis of the ruling class' claim to rule, resistance to that rule, whether to the immorality of economic subsidies and privileges, to the violation of the principle of equal treatment under equal law, or to its seizure of children's education, must deal with secularism's intellectual and moral core."[115]

So Where Are We with the Constitution?

This chapter is about the Constitution. But the point here is cultural. American culture has so far abandoned any adherence to the Constitution as a charter of limited government that there is scant

114 Angelo Codevilla, *The Ruling Class*, 49–50.
115 *Ibid.*, 73.

likelihood of appeals to the Constitution putting the brakes on the growing persecution of religion. Nevertheless, the educational and political effort must be made to reinstate, one by one, the now-discarded safeguards of liberty provided in the Constitution and to encourage the American people to recover the conviction that the most effective safeguard of liberty is a government of limited and specified powers. The ultimate answer, of course, is to be found in faith, fidelity, and prayer. In concluding his 2008 address at the John Paul II Institute, Cardinal Stafford said: "As *Humanae Vitae* with the whole Catholic tradition teaches, we are to be true with body and soul."

PART III.

AN UNACKNOWLEDGED CAUSE: CONTRACEPTION

Introduction

As noted in Part I, the Obama Regime has claimed a power superior to God: by compelling citizens, contrary to conscience, to violate the prohibitory law of God; and by overriding the decision of God to create human beings as only "male and female."[1] The ground was prepared for that claim by the progressive submission of the American people to the Dictatorship of Relativism in its various manifestations. Secularism, relativism, legal positivism, individualism, and the demotion of conscience to a subjective decision, all imply a displacement of the law of God as a binding moral imperative. Every society and every person has to have a god, an ultimate moral authority, whether it is the real God, the individual himself or some other. The Regime could not have pulled off its claim to ultimate authority if the American people had not confirmed their relativist displacement of God with the massive, and nearly universal, practice of contraception. In contraception, "they claim a power which belongs solely to God, the power to decide, *in a final analysis*, the coming into existence of a human person."[2] If the people claim that divine power for themselves, they put absolute authority up for grabs. Who can be surprised when the Regime makes its own claim and backs it up with its exclusive power of coercion? The Catholic Church must, and

1   Gen. 1:27.
2   John Paul II, Discourse, Sept. 17, 1983.

will, resist that claim of the State to ultimate moral as well as legal authority. The result will be, and already is, a persecution. The acceptance of contraception has been, and is, a material, though unacknowledged, cause of that persecution. In the succeeding chapters, let us consider why that is so and what can be done about it.

9. NINETEEN CENTURIES OF CONDEMNATION

Lambeth 1930

Until 1930, no Christian denomination had ever said that con-traception could ever be a moral choice. The 1908 Anglican Lambeth Conference reflected that unity and condemned contraception as "demoralizing to character and hostile to national welfare."[3]

The next Lambeth Conference, of 1930, reversed that position and stated that "in those cases where there is [a] clearly felt moral obligation to limit or avoid parenthood, and where there is a morally sound reason for avoiding complete abstinence, the Conference agrees that other methods may be used, provided that this is done in the light of the same Christian principles. The Conference [condemns] the use of any methods of birth control from selfishness, luxury or mere convenience."[4]

Since Lambeth 1930, Pius XI[5] and succeeding popes have maintained the traditional teaching, culminating in *Humanae Vitae*, the 1968 encyclical of Paul VI.

Not Just a Catholic Thing

"Contraception," wrote Fr. John Hardon, S.J., "goes back to the earliest days of recorded history . . . to as early as 2800 B.C."[6] Contraception is the prevention of life while abortion is the taking of life after it has begun.

---

3   See www.cafeanglican.org/view/sexuality/html.
4   *N.Y. Times*, Aug. 15, 1930, p. 1.
5   *Casti Connubii* (1931).
6   John A. Hardon, S.J., *The Catholic Family in the Modern World* (St. Paul, Minn.: Leaflet Missal Co., 1991), 1.

Opposition to contraception is not limited to the Catholic Church. Martin Luther "sharply condemned the contraceptive mentality that was alive and well in his time. . . . He linked both contraception and abortion to selfishness: 'How great, therefore, the wickedness of [fallen] human nature is! How many girls there are who prevent conception and kill and expel tender fetuses, although procreation is the work of God!'"[7]

"In the Onan account in *Gen.* 38:6–10 . . . Onan practices withdrawal, and God slays him because he has done an abominable thing. For twenty centuries, Christians recognized this as a teaching against contraception. . . . [W]e read in the first-century Didache a condemnation of contraception. . . . Luther, Calvin and Wesley and about 100 prominent Protestant theologians over the years interpreted the Onan account as a condemnation of contraceptive behavior. Luther called it a form of sodomy; Calvin called it a form of homicide."[8]

"It was Evangelicals who—starting in 1873—successfully built a web of federal and state laws that equated contraception and abortion, suppressed the spread of birth control information and devices, and even criminalized the use of contraceptives. And it was Evangelicals who attempted to jail early twentieth-century birth control crusaders such as Margaret Sanger."[9]

Serious Protestant voices now question the rejection of the traditional Christian teaching.[10] "The . . . separation of sex from procreation," said R. Albert Mohler, Jr., president of the Southern

---

7   Allan Carlson, "The Children of the Reformation," *Touchstone,* May 2007; Sam and Bethany Torode, *Open Embrace* (Grand Rapids, Mich.: Eerdmans, 2002), 62–63; see Allan Carlson, "The Ironic Protestant Reversal: How the Original Family Movement Swallowed the Pill," *Family Policy,* Volume 12, Number 5 (September/ October 1999): 16–21.

8   John F. Kippley, "Truth or Consequences," *Lay Witness,* June 1996, pp. 8, 26.

9   Allan Carlson, "Godly Seed: American Evangelicals Confront Birth Control (1873–1973), *Human Life Review,* Spring 2012, 5, 6.

10   See Charles Provan, *The Bible and Birth Control;* Russell Shorto, "Contra-Contraception," *N.Y. Times Magazine,* May 7, 2006, p. 49; Elizabeth Altham, "Converging Paths," *Sursum Corda* (Summer 1998), p. 60.

Baptist Theological Seminary, "may be one of the most important defining marks of our age—and one of the most ominous. . . . [T]he pill gave . . . license to everything from adultery and affairs to premarital sex and within marriage to a separation of the sex act and procreation."[11]

So Why is Contraception Wrong?

As spelled out in papal statements, contraception is wrong for three reasons:

1. *Contraception deliberately separates the unitive and procreative aspects of the conjugal act.*

In *Humanae Vitae*, Pope Paul VI said that the law of God prohibits "every action which, either in anticipation of the conjugal act, or in its accomplishment, or in the development of its natural consequences, aims, whether as an end or as a means, at making procreation impossible."[12] This teaching "is founded upon the inseparable connection—which is willed by God and which man cannot lawfully break on his own initiative—between the two meanings of the conjugal act: the unitive and the procreative meanings."[13]

In *Letter to Families*, John Paul II said: "[T]he moment in which a man and a woman, uniting themselves in one flesh, can become parents . . . is a moment of special value both for their interpersonal relationship and for their service to life: They can become parents—father and mother—by communicating life to a new human being. The two dimensions of conjugal union, the unitive and procreative, cannot be artificially separated without damaging the deepest truth of the conjugal act itself."[14]

---

11 Russell Shorto, "Contra-Contraception," *New York Times Magazine*, May 7, 2006, pp. 46, 50, 55.
12 *HV*, no. 14.
13 *Ibid.*, no. 12.
14 *LTF*, no. 12.

2. *The acceptance of contraception asserts that man, rather than God, is the arbiter of whether and, if so, when human life shall begin.*

Contraception is a First Commandment issue: Who is God? "At the origin of every human person there is a creative act of God. . . . [T]he procreative capacity, inscribed in human sexuality is . . . a cooperation with God's creative power. [M]en and women are not the arbiters . . . of this . . . capacity, called as they are, in it and through it, to be participants in God's creative decision. When . . . through contraception, married couples remove from the exercise of their conjugal sexuality its potential procreative capacity, they claim a power which belongs solely to God: the power to decide, in *a final analysis*, the coming into existence of a human person. They assume the qualification not of being cooperators in God's creative power, but the ultimate depositaries of the source of human life."[15]

The only creating God has done since *Genesis* is the creation of each individual, spiritual human soul. When you put a male and a female dog together, the material forces operate and you get a litter of puppies. But a spiritual soul cannot be generated this way. As Benedict XVI said at the Mass for the inauguration of his pontificate: "We are not some casual and meaningless product of evolution. Each of us is the result of a thought of God. Each of us is willed, each of us is loved, each of us is necessary."[16] God has chosen to depend on human cooperation for the creation of new citizens for the kingdom of heaven. The contracepting couple reject that gift by altering the conjugal act to prevent that creation. What they say to God is something like this: "For all we know, God, it may be your will that from this act of ours a new person will come into existence who will live forever. For all we know, that may be your will. And we won't let you do it." That is awesome. "Contraception," said John Paul II, "is so profoundly

15 Pope John Paul II, *Discourse*, Sept. 17, 1983; 28 *The Pope Speaks* 356–57 (1983).
16 Pope Benedict XVI, Homily, April 24, 2005.

unlawful as never to be, for any reason, justified. To think or to say the contrary is equal to maintaining that in human life situations may arise in which it is lawful not to recognize God as God."[17]

3. *Contraception destroys the mutual self-donation which ought to characterize the conjugal act.*

As John Paul II explained, God, who is love, "wills" that each human person ought to come into existence through a loving act of self-gift between spouses united in a "communion of persons . . . drawn . . . from the mystery of the Trinitarian *we*."[18] The conjugal act, therefore, is an image of the self-giving relation of the persons of the Trinity.

Contraception is degrading to the persons who practice it and to the integrity of the spousal relationship.[19] John Paul made this point:

> When couples, by . . . contraception, separate these two meanings that God . . . has inscribed in . . . their sexual communion, they act as "arbiters" of the divine plan and they "manipulate" and degrade human sexuality and with it themselves and their married partner by altering its value of "total" self-giving. [T]he innate language that expresses the total reciprocal self-giving of husband and wife is overlaid through contraception by [a] contradictory language . . . of not giving oneself totally to the other. This leads not only to a . . . refusal to be open to life but also to a falsification of the . . . truth of conjugal love, which is called upon to give itself in personal totality.[20]

Contraception transforms the conjugal act from an act of total

17 Pope John Paul II, *Discourse*, Sept. 17, 1983.
18 *LTF*, no. 8.
19 See John F. Crosby, "The Mystery of 'Fair Love,'" *Catholic World Report*, Apr. 1999, 52, 57.
20 Pope John Paul II, *FC*, no. 32.

self-donation to a mutual pursuit of self-gratification.[21] It becomes, in effect, mutual masturbation. Contraception also accepts the idea that there is such a thing as a life not worth living—the life that would come into existence but for their refusal to cooperate in his (or her) creation.

An Unchanging Truth

"Forty years after its publication," said Benedict XVI, *Humanae Vitae* "reveals [its] farsightedness. . . . The truth expressed in [HV] does not change; on the contrary, precisely in the light of the new scientific discoveries, its teaching becomes more timely and elicits reflection on [its] intrinsic value. . . . The urgent need for education . . . primarily concerns the theme of life. I . . . hope that young people . . . will be given very special attention so that they may learn the true meaning of love and prepare for it . . . without [being] distracted by ephemeral messages that prevent them from reaching the essence of the truth at stake. . . . The teaching expressed by [HV] conforms with the fundamental structure through which life has always been transmitted since the world's creation, with respect for nature and . . . its needs."[22]

What about Natural Family Planning (NFP)?

NFP does not mean "Not for Protestants." It is rooted in nature. In NFP, the couple refrain from sexual relations during the few days of the month in which the woman is fertile. When they engage in relations during the rest of the month, they may prefer not to have a child. But they have an accepting intent, in that they do not destroy the integrity of the act and they are willing to accept the responsibility for a child. The contracepting couple may be willing to accept a child if one results from their act. But they

---

21 See Scott Hahn, "Sex, Lies and Sacraments," *CCC Family Foundations* (Couple to Couple League), May-June 1999, 4.
22 Pope Benedict XVI, *Address*, May 10, 2008.

take measures, by drugs or plugs, to destroy the integrity of the act to prevent a child. The privilege of procreation, however, is so important that NFP can be used only if "there are serious motives to space out births."[23] What motives are sufficient will depend on circumstances. The advice of a prudent priest can be essential. "Uniquely important in this field is unity of moral and pastoral judgment by priests."[24]

NFP and contraception, said John Paul, involve "two irreconcilable concepts of the human person and of human sexuality. The choice of the natural rhythms involves accepting the cycle of . . . the woman, and . . . accepting dialogue. . . respect, shared responsibility, and self-control. To accept the cycle and enter into dialogue means to recognize both the spiritual and corporal character of conjugal communion and to live personal love with its requirement of fidelity."[25]

"In destroying the power of giving life through contraception," said Mother Teresa at the 1994 National Prayer Breakfast, "a husband or wife . . . turns the attention to self and so destroys the gift of love. . . . The husband and wife must turn the attention to each other, as . . . in natural family planning and not to self, as . . . in contraception. Once that living love is destroyed by contraception, abortion follows very easily."[26]

A War of Cultures

The United States Conference of Catholic Bishops in 2006 described well the contrast between the contraceptive culture and the rich and hope-filled teaching of the Church: "Our culture," the statement said, "presents sex as merely recreational, not as a deeply personal . . . encounter between spouses. In this view, being responsible about sex . . . means limiting its consequences—avoiding disease and using contraceptives to prevent pregnancy. This

23 Pope Paul VI, *Humanae Vitae*, no. 16.
24 Pope John Paul II, FC, no. 34.
25 Pope John Paul II, *Familiaris Consortio*, no. 32.
26 *Family Resource Center News*, May 1994, p. 13.

cultural view is impoverished, even sad. It fails to account for the true needs and deepest desires of men and women. Living in accord with this view has caused much loneliness and many broken hearts. God's plan for married life and love is far richer and more fulfilling. . . . The total giving of oneself, body and soul, to one's beloved, is no time to say: 'I give you everything I am—except. . . . ' The Church's teaching is not only about observing a rule, but about preserving that total mutual gift of two persons in its integrity. This may seem a hard saying. . . . But as many couples who have turned away from contraception tell us, living this teaching can contribute to the honesty, openness and intimacy of marriage and help make couples truly fulfilled."[27]

27   USCCB, *Married Love and the Gift of Life*, Nov. 14, 2006.

10. CONSEQUENCES

Opponents of . . . same-sex marriage [are] a little late. The walls of traditional marriage were breached 40 years ago; what we are witnessing now is the storming of the last bastion. . . . Since the invention of the Pill . . . human beings have for the first time been able to control reproduction. . . . The impulse toward premarital chastity for women was always the fear of bearing a child alone. The Pill removed this fear. Along with it went the need of men to commit themselves exclusively to one woman . . . to enjoy sexual relations at all. Over the past four decades, women have trained men that marriage is no longer necessary for sex. But women have also sadly discovered that they can't reliably gain men's sexual and emotional commitment to them by giving them sex before marriage. . . .

Men and women living together and having sexual relations . . . became . . . the dominant lifestyle in the under-30 demographic within the past few years. . . . When society decided—and we have decided, this fight is over—that society would no longer decide the legitimacy of sexual relations between particular men and women, weddings became . . . symbolic . . . the shortcut way to make the legal compact regarding property rights, inheritance and . . . other . . . benefits. But what weddings do not do any longer is give to a man and a woman society's permission to have sex and procreate.

Sex, childbearing and marriage now have no necessary connection to one another, because the biological connection between sex and childbearing is controllable. . . . If society has abandoned regulating heterosexual conduct . . . what right does it have to regulate homosexual conduct, including the regulation of their legal . . . relationship . . . to mirror exactly that of hetero, married couples? I believe that this state of affairs is contrary to the will of God. But traditionalists, especially Christian traditionalists . . . need to . . . face the fact that same-sex marriage . . . will not *cause* the degeneration of . . . marriage; it is the *result* of it. *Pastor Donald Sensing, Trinity United Methodist Church, Franklin, TN.*[28]

When the Federal Council of Churches in 1931 followed Lambeth by endorsing "careful and restrained" use of contraceptives, the *Washington Post* responded in an editorial that was, in effect, a lament for a Protestant culture sliding into the moral incoherence intrinsic to the principle of private interpretation: "It is impossible to reconcile . . . the divine institution of marriage with . . . the mechanical regulation or suppression of . . . birth. The church must either reject the . . . Bible or reject . . . the 'scientific' production of human souls. Carried to its logical conclusion, the committee's report [approving contraceptives] . . . would sound the death-knell of marriage . . . by establishing degrading practices which would encourage indiscriminate immorality. The suggestion that the use of legalized contraceptives would be 'careful and restrained' is preposterous."[29]

After Lambeth 1930, nothing much happened until the 1960s. With the advent of the Pill, the ground shifted. Francis Fukuyama called the introduction of the Pill "the Great Disruption in relations between men and women."[30] By 2012, social science

28 Donald Sensing, "Save Marriage? It's Too Late," *Wall Street Journal, Opinion Journal*, March 15, 2004.
29 *Washington Post*, editorial, March 22, 1931.
30 Francis Fukuyama, *The Great Disruption: Human Nature and the Reconstitution of the Social Order* (1999), 101–03, 120–22.

researcher Mary Eberstadt concluded that "[c]ontraceptive sex is the fundamental social fact of our time."[31]

Humanae Vitae Nailed It

Events have validated Pope Paul's prediction that the acceptance of contraception would lead to "conjugal infidelity and the general lowering of morality," a loss of "respect" for women, and the placing of "a dangerous weapon . . . in the hands of . . . public authorities."[32] As Archbishop Charles Chaput put it: "If Paul VI were right about so many of the consequences deriving from contraception, it is because he was right about contraception itself."[33]

Two decades before *Humanae Vitae*, Dean William J. Kenealy, S.J., of Boston College Law School, whom I was privileged to have as a Jurisprudence teacher, testified in favor of the Massachusetts laws restricting the distribution of contraceptives. "If a person can violate [by contraception] the natural integrity of the marriage act with moral impunity," said Fr. Kenealy, "then I challenge anyone to show me the essential immorality of any sexual aberration."[34] Like Paul VI, Fr. Kenealy had it right. Let's look briefly at some consequences of contraception:

Demographics. *Roe v. Wade* legalized abortion in 1973. From 1973 through 2011, 54,559,615 unborn children were killed by surgical abortion in the United States.[35] This does not include the undoubtedly much larger number killed by chemical and other early abortifacients including "contraceptives" which prevent the new human being from implanting in the womb. Nor does it include the incalculable numbers of persons denied existence by contraception. The shortage of people caused by contraception

31 Mary Eberstadt, *Adam and Eve After the Pill* (2012), 15, 136.
32 *HV*, no. 17.
33 Archbishop Charles Chaput, OFM Cap., Pastoral Letter, "On Human Life," July 22, 1998.
34 William J. Kenealy, S.J., "The Birth Control Issue in Massachusetts," 46 *Catholic Mind* (1948), 11.
35 National Right to Life Educational Trust Fund, www.nrlc.org; Guttmacher Institute, Fact Sheet, July 2013. www.guttmacher.org.

and abortion affects the economy, education, and election results among other effects. This "birth dearth" afflicts non-Muslim countries throughout the world and especially in formerly Christian Europe.[36] In the United States, contraception has been a "clear factor in the decline of the Catholic community."[36] "A stranger came into the sacristy after Mass," wrote Fr. Timothy Sauppé of Peoria. "In an incriminating huff he said, 'I have been away from the area for fifteen years; where are the people? And now you are tearing down the school? I went there as a kid.' . . . I calmly said, 'Let me ask you a question: How many kids did you have?' He said, 'Two.' Then I said, 'So did everyone else. When you only have two kids per family there is no growth.' His demeanor changed, and then he dropped his head and said, 'And they aren't even going to Mass anymore.'"[38]

Abortion. If, through contraception, one makes himself (or herself) the arbiter of whether and when life begins, he will predictably make himself the arbiter of when it shall end. A contraceptive society requires abortion as a backup for failed contraception. Pope John Paul stated that "the pro-abortion culture is . . . strong . . . where the Church's teaching on contraception is rejected. . . . [C]ontraception and abortion are . . . different evils; . . . . But contraception and abortion are . . . fruits of the same tree. . . . [I]n many cases contraception and even abortion are practiced under the pressure of real-life difficulties, which . . . can never exonerate from striving to observe God's law fully . . . [I]n very many other instances such practices are rooted in a hedonistic mentality . . . and they imply a self-centered concept of freedom, which regards procreation as an obstacle to personal fulfillment. The life which could result from a sexual encounter thus becomes an enemy . . . and abortion becomes the only possible decisive response to contraception. The close connection between . . . contraception and . . .

36 For statistics and analyses, see Population Research Institute, PO Box 1559, Front Royal, VA 22630.
37 Bishop Alexander Sample of Marquette, MI, Lifesitenews.com, Dec. 7, 2011.
38 Bellarmine Forum, May 14, 2013; www.bellarmineforum.org.

abortion . . . is . . . demonstrated . . . by the . . . chemical products, intrauterine devices and vaccines which, distributed with the same ease as contraceptives . . . act as abortifacients in the very early stages of . . . the life of the new human being."[39]

Euthanasia. Contraception and abortion have left the United States with a diminished pool of workers to support the elderly, sick, and disabled. Contraception and abortion accustomed people to the idea that some lives are not worth bringing into existence or continuing in existence. This clears the way for rationing of health care and euthanasia of those whose lives are considered "useless."[40] In our culture the intentional killing of the innocent is widely seen as an optional problem-solving technique, as in Columbine and other mass shootings. Legalized abortion is the clearest example. Another is informal euthanasia. In the Terri Schiavo case, the judge ordered the removal of nutrition and hydration from a disabled woman who was not dying and was not in significant pain. It was a judicially decreed execution. That result is duplicated without public awareness in the many cases where the family and caregivers agree to remove food and water because they think it would be better for the patient to die.[41] Contraception, abortion, and euthanasia all manifest a utilitarian approach to the beginning and the termination of life.

Pornography. Pope Paul, in *Humanae Vitae*, warned that contraception would cause women to be viewed as objects, that "man . . . may come to the point of considering her as a mere instrument of selfish enjoyment and no longer as his respected and beloved companion." Contraception reduces the conjugal act to a temporary alliance for individual satisfaction—what Paul VI called "the juxtaposition of two solitudes."[42]

---

39 *EV*, nos. 13, 15.
40 See 30 *Origins* 194 (2000), describing the authorization of federal funding of research on "human embryonic stem cells," which involves the killing of innocent human beings for the possible benefit of others.
41 See Charles E. Rice and Theresa Farnan, *Where did I come from? Where am I going? How do I get there?* (2009), 187–91.
42 "Conversations with Pope Paul VI," *McCall's*, Oct. 1967, 93, 138.

Pornography is the separation of sex from life and the reduction of sex to an exercise in self-gratification. In the process, a woman, or a child in child pornography, becomes an object rather than a person.

Promiscuity. One reason why sex is reserved for marriage is that sex inherently has something to do with babies and the natural way to raise children is in a marriage. But if it is entirely up to us to decide whether sex will have anything to do with babies, why should it be reserved for marriage?

Divorce. One reason, in the nature of things, why marriage should be permanent, is that sex is inherently related to procreation and the natural way to raise children is in a home with parents permanently married to each other. But if sex and marriage are not intrinsically related to the generation of children, then marriage loses its reason for permanence.

Homosexual Activity. The contraceptive society cannot deny legitimacy to the homosexual lifestyle without denying its own premise, that whether sex will have any relation to procreation is entirely up to the decision of the persons involved. When same-sex "marriage" is proposed, the response of contraceptionist defenders of traditional marriage will emphasize utilitarian arguments, e.g., whether same-sex marriage "works," whether it is good for any children involved, etc. This trivializes the issues. The homosexualization of our culture and law[43] is the most ominous result of the acceptance of contraception. That homosexualization involves the rejection of reason as well as God and it clears the way for the State as the absolute authority to control the family and virtually every aspect of human existence.

In Vitro Fertilization.[44] IVF is the flip side of contraception. IVF engineers procreation without sexual union, while contraception seeks to take the unitive without the procreative. In IVF, the

43 See Chapters 3, 4 and 7.
44 See discussion in John-Henry Westen, Interview with Bishop Ignacio Carrasco de Paula, President, Pontifical Academy for Life, LifeSiteNews.com, Sept. 11, 2013.

egg is fertilized outside the womb ("in vitro") and then implanted in the womb and carried to birth if the intent is to have the birth of a child. Usually excess eggs are fertilized. The extra embryos, who are living human beings, are frozen or used for research. See the discussion of cloning below.

Cloning. Dolly, the cloned sheep, was introduced to the world in 1997 by Dr. Ian Wilmut in Edinburgh. Dr. Wilmut took from an adult "donor" sheep a cell which he treated so that all its genes could be activated so as to develop into a lamb. He electrically fused that cell with the unfertilized egg of a ewe, from which egg the nucleus containing the DNA of the ewe had been removed. The fused cell and egg interacted and developed into a lamb embryo. Since the ewe's DNA had been removed, the only DNA in the embryo was that of the "donor." The embryo was then implanted in a "surrogate mother" sheep and carried to term. The result is Dolly, a sheep that is a genetic copy of the "donor" sheep. The cloning process is called somatic cell nuclear transfer (SCNT). If the cloned embryo is implanted in a womb and carried to term, it is called reproductive cloning. If cloned embryos are grown for several days and then destroyed to create embryonic stem cell lines for the supposed (but to date unsubstantiated) purpose of treating genetic and other disorders, it is called therapeutic cloning. Problematic success has been reported in the therapeutic cloning of human embryos.[45] The "therapeutic" use of embryonic stem cells involves the destruction of the embryo. That is, in the moral sense, murder whether that embryo was created by IVF or cloning. Efforts in Congress to ban cloning and to ban federal funding of embryonic stem cell research have had limited success.[46] Once the acceptance of contraception severed the link between sexual intercourse and procreation, the generation of human life inevitably became a laboratory project with no intrinsic limit on such projects.

---

45 Wesley J. Smith, "The Arrival of Human Cloning," *The Weekly Standard*, May 27, 2013, p. 20.
46 *Ibid.*

Summary

The practice of contraception presents a First Commandment problem: Who is God? The real God or the autonomous individual deciding whether he (or she) will permit human life to begin? That is about as basic as it gets.

11. A FIRST COMMANDMENT ISSUE

I am the LORD your God: you shall not have strange Gods before me. — *First Commandment*[47]

"[T]he single principal cause for the breakdown of the Catholic faith in materially overdeveloped countries like ours," said Fr. John Hardon, S.J., "has been contraception. St. James tells us that faith without good works is dead. What good is it to give verbal profession of the Catholic faith, and then behave like a pagan in marital morality?"[48]

"When . . . , through contraception," it bears repeating,[49] "married couples remove from the exercise of their conjugal sexuality its potential procreative capacity, they claim a power which belongs solely to God: the power to decide, *in a final analysis*, the coming into existence of a human person."[50] "Contraception," said John Paul, "is so profoundly unlawful as never to be, for any reason, justified. To think or to say the contrary is equal to maintaining that in human life situations may arise in which it is lawful not to recognize God as God."[51]

Catholics practice contraception at about the same rate as everyone else.[52] It is unlikely that many, if any, Catholics using contraception consciously interpret that act as a refusal "to recognize God as God." The analysis of contraception as an objective evil implies no judgment on the subjective culpability of those

---

47 CCC, no. 2052; Ex 20:2–17; Deut. 5:6–21.
48 John A. Hardon, S.J., "Contraception: Fatal to the Faith, and to Eternal Life," *Eternal Life*, April 19, 1999, 27, 29.
49 See Chapters 9 and 10.
50 Pope John Paul II, Discourse, Sept. 17, 1983.
51 *Ibid.*
52 See Frank Newport, "Americans, Including Catholics, Say Birth Control is Morally OK," www.galluppoll, May 22, 2012.

practicing it. Subjective culpability requires knowledge that the act is wrong and the intent to do it.[53] John Paul's analysis, however, is right on the money. Contraception is the seizure of the prerogative of God. Nor is contraception the only area from which the law of God is consciously or unconsciously excluded. Economic neoliberalism in America, as described by John Paul II,[54] and political activity[55] provide ready examples. Another is the liberation of science from moral norms. In contraception, the parties do not presume to change the physical or other characteristics of any new persons they might permit God to create. In wrongful genetic manipulation, however, that is precisely the object.

Designer Babies

Over the past two decades, the idea of engineering new babies according to genetic specification has moved from science fiction to reality.[56] In 2002, Cardinal Joseph Ratzinger, later Benedict XVI, addressed this problem and struck a balance between the use of science for healing and its improper use to make man the God of the terms on which human life may begin.

"As long as this [artificial reassembling of genes] is done for the purpose of healing, and with due reverence for creation," Ratzinger said, "it is good. To the extent that man believes himself . . . to be . . . a co-creator . . . an engineer of the world, he can . . . become a destroyer of life. . . . [E]ven the beginning of genetic manipulation is liable to develop into an assumption of domination over the world, which will then carry within it the seeds of destruction. Man is incapable of creating anything; he can only reassemble things. . . . [H]e can become an assistant and keeper in God's garden. But wherever he puts himself forward as maker of things himself, then creation is threatened."

Cardinal Ratzinger went on to place the problem in the

53 See CCC, no. 1860.
54 EA, no. 56.
55 VS, no. 101.
56 The Embryo Project Encyclopedia, www.embryo.asu.edu.

context of *Genesis* 3 and the posting of angels east of Eden with flaming swords to keep man, after the Fall, from eating of the Tree of Life. After the Fall, man was forbidden to eat of that tree which gave immortality, "since to be immortal in this [fallen] condition would . . . be perdition." People, "with genetic codes available to them," are now, Ratzinger said, "starting to pick from the tree of life and make themselves lords of life and death, to reassemble life. . . . [P]recisely what man was supposed to be protected from is now . . . happening: he is crossing the final boundary. . . . [M]an makes other men his own artifacts. Man no longer originates in the mystery of love, by . . . conception and birth . . . but is produced industrially, like any other product. . . . [We] can . . . be certain of this: God will take action to counter an ultimate crime, an ultimate act of self-destruction, on the part of man. He will take action against the attempt to demean mankind by the production of slave-beings. There are indeed final boundaries we cannot cross without turning into the agents of the destruction of creation itself, without going far beyond the original sin and the first Fall and all its negative consequences."[57]

The Homosexual State as God

The most direct and most logical consequence of the acceptance of contraception is the validation of the homosexual separation of sex from procreation. That validation of the homosexual lifestyle includes the nullification of God's original creation of human beings as male and female[58] and his establishment of the family based on the permanent union of one man and one woman.[59] "Neither the church nor the state 'own' the institution of marriage," said Cardinal Francis George. "The state has a right to supervise but not to redefine an institution it did not create. This tendency for the government to claim for itself authority over all

57 Joseph Cardinal Ratzinger, *God and the World* (2002), 132–35.
58 Gen 1:27.
59 Mt 19:3–9; Mk:10:2–12.

areas of human experience flows from the secularization of our culture. If God cannot be a part of public life, then the state itself plays God. There are many paths to total state control of life—fascism, totalitarianism, communism. In the United States, the path is labeled protection of individual human rights."[60]

In this broad and deep homosexualization of law and culture, the State is neither a spectator nor a referee. It is rather the initiator and enforcer of a legal and cultural revolution. In the armed forces, education, and the workplace, the Obama Administration actively promotes the homosexual agenda. For example, on July 24, 2013, the Arcadia, California school district submitted to demands by the Obama Department of Justice and agreed to a settlement "allowing an incoming high school freshman who is anatomically female but identifies as a boy to use the restroom and changing facilities assigned to her preferred sex, rather than her biological sex. . . . The Obama administration pressured the school district to allow the girl to use the boys' facilities, saying in a letter that failure to do so constitutes sexual discrimination 'against students who do not conform to sex stereotypes.'"[61]

Empowerment of the homosexual agenda is becoming routine at every level of government. On August 13, 2013, Governor Jerry Brown "signed California's new 'transgender' law, making that state the fifth where it is legal for self-identifying 'transgender' children to use bathrooms, showers, locker rooms, and changing rooms designated for children of the opposite biological sex. 'Now, every transgender student in California will be able to get up in the morning knowing that when they go to school as their authentic self they will have the same fair chance at success as their classmates,' said Mason Davis, Executive Director of the Transgender Law Center."[62]

In states where same-sex "marriage" is legalized, and even

60 "The Cardinal's Column," *Catholic New World*, June 9-June 22, 2013.
61 LifeSiteNews, July 25, 2013.
62 LifeSiteNews, Aug. 13, 2013.

where it is not,[63] Christian florists, photographers, and meeting room proprietors have been charged with, or convicted of, violating state law by refusing to provide their services or facilities for a "gay" wedding.[64] "If you look at other nations that have gone down the road towards gay marriage," said Senator Ted Cruz (R-TX), prosecution for hate speech is "the next step [where] [i]t gets enforced against Christian pastors who decline to perform gay marriages, who speak out and preach biblical truths on marriage."[65]

The Basic Conflict

We could multiply anecdotal references to the ways in which the enforcement of "gender neutrality" will infringe upon religious freedom, the rights of conscience, and family integrity, as predicted by Archbishop John Myers.[66] The point here, rather, is to address the basic conflict. In its enforcement of the homosexual agenda, the secularistic State offers no quarter. Its main targets are the family—and God. Which means that its uncompromising foe on earth is the Catholic Church because it is the Body of Christ who is God.

The family is the first target. In *Lumen Fidei*, his first encyclical, which adapted the draft prepared by Benedict XVI, Pope Francis affirmed the primacy of the family: "The first setting in which faith enlightens the human city is the family. I think first and foremost of the stable union of man and woman in marriage. This union is born of their love, as a sign . . . of God's own love, and of the . . . acceptance of the goodness of sexual differentiation, whereby spouses can become one flesh (cf. *Gen* 2:24) and are enabled to give birth to a new life, a manifestation of the Creator's goodness, wisdom and loving plan. Grounded in this love, a man

63 See *Elane Photography v. Willock*, Supreme Court of New Mexico, Docket No. 33, 687, Aug. 22, 2013.
64 LifeSiteNews.com, Aug. 12, 2013.
65 LifeSiteNews, July 24, 2013.
66 See Chapter 3.

and a woman can promise each other mutual love in a gesture which engages their entire lives and mirrors many features of faith. Promising love for ever is possible when we perceive a plan bigger than our own ideas and undertakings, a plan which sustains us and enables us to surrender our future entirely to the one we love. Faith also helps us to grasp in all its depth and richness the begetting of children, as a sign of the love of the Creator who entrusts us with the mystery of a new person."[67]

In speaking against the (ultimately successful) proposal by the Argentine government to legalize same-sex "marriage," Cardinal Jorge Mario Bergoglio (now Pope Francis) spelled out what is at stake on that issue. And he flatly labeled the proposal "a 'move' of the father of lies":

> At stake is the identity and survival of the family: father, mother and children. At stake are the lives of many children who will be discriminated against in advance, and deprived of their human development given by a father and a mother and willed by God. At stake is the total rejection of God's law engraved in our hearts. . . . [T]his is . . . an attempt to destroy God's plan. It is a 'move' of the father of lies who seeks to confuse and deceive the children of God.[68]

Over the centuries, many causes have led to persecutions of the Church. Obviously, contraception is not a usual cause of persecution. The point of this book, however, is that the seismic undermining of moral Truth that occurred at Lambeth 1930 precipitated, with the advent of the Pill in the 1960s, a practically universal abandonment of that Truth. That displacement of the Divine Law as a normative measure of conduct affected every moral issue and invited the State to fill the vacuum by establishing its will as the criterion of morality as well as of law. The people cannot be automatically blamed for this because they were

67 Pope Francis, *LF*, no. 52.
68 *National Catholic Register*, July 8, 2010.

deprived, over four decades and more, of any coherent exposition of the positive and hope-filled teaching of the Catholic Church on marriage, the family, and the transmission of life.

We are in this fix because of the abdication by most bishops of their responsibility to teach and lead over the past few decades. The bishops themselves have admitted their failure to explain *Humanae Vitae* and other matters. That admission itself was an act of courage. We outline the dimensions of their acknowledged failure of leadership, not to criticize them but to encourage them in their return to renewed efforts to do their job. And we emphasize that they are entitled to our support and prayer.

12. A TEACHING UNTAUGHT

Doesn't the Church have a problem conveying its moral principles to its own flock? "Do we ever!" the archbishop replies with a hearty laugh. "I'm not afraid to admit that we have an internal catechetical challenge—a towering one—in convincing our own people of the moral beauty and coherence of what we teach. That's a biggie"

For this he faults the church leadership. "We have gotten gun-shy . . . in speaking with any amount of cogency on chastity and sexual morality." He dates this diffidence to "the mid- and late-'60s, when the whole world seemed to be caving in, and where Catholics in general got the impression that what the Second Vatican Council taught, first and foremost, is that we should be chums with the world, and that the best thing the Church can do is become more and more like everybody else."

The "flash point," the archbishop says, was *Humanae Vitae*, Pope Paul VI's 1968 encyclical reasserting the Church's teaching on sex, marriage and reproduction, including its opposition to artificial contraception. It "brought such a tsunami of dissent, departure, disapproval of the church, that I think most of us—and I'm using the first-person plural intentionally, including myself—kind of subconsciously said, 'Whoa. We'd better never talk about that, because it's just too hot to handle.' We forfeited the chance to be a coherent moral voice when it comes to one of the more burning issues of the day."

Without my having raised the subject, he adds that the Church's sex-abuse scandal "intensified our laryngitis over speaking about issues of chastity and sexual morality because we almost thought, 'I'll blush if I do. . . . After what some priests and some bishops, albeit a tiny minority, have done, how will I have any credibility in speaking on that?'" — Interview of Cardinal Timothy Dolan, President, USCCB.[69]

Such an admission by the nation's leading bishop of dereliction of duty on the part of himself and his brother bishops is unprecedented. Cardinal Dolan acknowledged the hunger, especially among young adults, for a more authoritative Church voice on sexuality: "They will be quick to say, 'By the way, we want you to know that we might not be able to obey it. . . . But we want to hear it. And in justice you as our pastors need to tell us, and you need to challenge us.'"[70] But the Cardinal offered no clue as to whether and when the American Church will provide that voice.

That failure to teach did not spring from nowhere. "Americanism," wrote Russell Shaw, former director of media relations for the USCCB, "understood in a broad sense as signifying Catholic assimilation into the secular culture, has been the dominant current in American Catholicism for many years."[71] The debate over the extent to which the Church should adapt to American culture has gone on since the mid-1800s.[72]

Catholic bishops and the bureaucracy in the USCCB have drawn justified criticism over decades for their promotion of a

69 James Taranto, "When the Archbishop Met the President," *Wall St. Journal Weekend Interview*, March 31, 2012.
70 *Ibid.*
71 Russell Shaw, "The Weathercock and the Mystic: The prophetic friendship of Orestes Brownson and Isaac Hecker," *Crisis*, July 24, 2006.
72 See Joseph Varacalli, *The Catholic Experience in America* (2005); Russell Shaw, *American Church* (2013); George Weigel, "Catholic 'Americanism,'" *National Review Online*, May 31, 2012.

liberal political agenda.[73] The facetious description of the bishops' bureaucracy as "the Democratic party at prayer" has a clear ring of truth. "At every turn in American politics since [the 1930s]," wrote Hillsdale College Professor Paul A. Rahe, "you will find the hierarchy assisting the Democratic Party and promoting the growth of the administrative entitlement state. . . . It did not cross the minds of those prelates that the liberty of conscience which they had grown to cherish is part of a larger package—that the paternalistic state, which recognizes no legitimate limits on its power and scope, that they had embraced would someday turn on the Church and seek to dictate whom it chose to teach its doctrines and how, more generally, it would conduct its affairs."[74]

An appearance, if not an obvious reality, of impropriety arises from the bishops' persistent support for the political agenda of the Ruling Class[75] combined with the receipt by agencies of the bishops of large governmental subsidies. For example, in 2011 the nationwide network of Catholic Charities had total "system" income of $4,600,193,411.00. Of that total, $2,944,123,783.04, or 64%, was "government revenue."[76]

The bishops now protest—rightly and admirably—against the Health Care Mandate, an enforcement of Obamacare that was readily foreseeable. But without the active support of the bishops and their bureaucracy, Obamacare would not have been enacted. Obamacare was enacted against the manifest will of the American people, in disregard of legislative process and by a level of bribery, coercion, and deception that was as open as it was unprecedented. Some bishops, to their credit, denounced Obamacare before its enactment, raising the obvious problems of centralization, infringement on liberty and cost.[77] But the

73 See Paul A. Rahe, "American Catholicism's Pact with the Devil," richocet.com, Feb. 10, 2012; Paul A. Rahe, "American Catholicism: A Call to Arms," richocet.com, Feb. 14, 2012.
74 Paul A. Rahe, "American Catholicism's Pact with the Devil," *ibid.*
75 See Chapter 8.
76 www.scribd.com/doc/117497900/Annual-Survey-2011-OVERVIEW.
77 See Joint Pastoral Statement of Archbishop Joseph F. Naumann and Bishop

USCCB itself was decisive in obtaining enactment of Obamacare through a practically exclusive focus on abortion, conscience, euthanasia, and immigration, while remaining silent about Obamacare's already obvious violations of liberty, subsidiarity and, incidentally, the Constitution. The bishops gave a free pass to Obamacare's massive violation of the principle of subsidiarity, its infringement on personal freedom and its potential for uncharted abuse capsulized by Nancy Pelosi's remark that "[W]e have to pass the bill so we can find out what is in it, away from the fog of the controversy."[78] On October 12, 2011, the USCCB's Committee on Pro-Life Activities, in urging legislation to protect conscience rights and prevent federal funding of abortion, nevertheless said that "with the passage of [Obamacare], our country took an important step toward ensuring access to health coverage for all Americans."[79] Such a benign description of Obamacare, even in 2011, is beyond delusional. It makes you wonder whether some bishops could possibly still believe that, even now.

The Catholic bishops helped to get us into this mess—the assault by the Obama Regime on religious liberty and the family. They have a special duty to try to get us out of it. The immediate problem, to borrow Cardinal Dolan's phrase, is the bishops' forfeiture of "the chance to be a coherent moral voice" with respect to *Humanae Vitae*. After the Lambeth Conference of 1930, the contraception issue lay dormant until the licensing of the Pill in the 1960s. When Paul VI issued *Humanae Vitae* in 1968, it was widely rejected. That same year, Cardinal Patrick O'Boyle of Washington, D.C., penalized nineteen priests for their public dissent from *Humanae Vitae*. Three years later, the Vatican ordered Cardinal O'Boyle to lift canonical penalties from those priests

Robert W. Finn, Sept. 1, 2009; see LifeSiteNews.com, Sept. 1, 2009, discussing statements by Bishop Walker Nickless of Sioux City, Iowa and Bishop Samuel J. Aquila of Fargo, North Dakota.

78 *The American Thinker*, Feb. 17, 2012.

79 USCCD Committee on Pro-Life Activities, letter of Cardinal Daniel N. DeNardo to Members of Congress, October 12, 2011.

who told him privately that they agreed that the teaching on "the objective evil of contraception" was "an authentic expression of [the] magisterium." The Vatican explicitly refrained from requiring that priests who had dissented publicly must retract their dissent publicly. That decision not to impose canonical penalties on openly dissenting priests came to be known as the Truce of 1968. As described by George Weigel:

> What I did argue in my 2002 book, *The Courage to be Catholic,* and what I would still argue today, is that the Truce of 1968 (exemplified by the settlement of the Washington Case) taught various lessons to various sectors of the Church in America.
>
> The Truce of 1968 taught theologians, priests and other Church professionals that dissent from authoritative teaching was, essentially, cost-free.
>
> The Truce of 1968 taught bishops inclined to defend authoritative Catholic teaching vigorously that they should think twice about doing so, if controversy were likely to follow; Rome, fearing schism, was nervous about public action against dissent. The result . . . was that "a generation of Catholic bishops came to think of themselves less as authoritative teachers than as moderators of an ongoing dialogue whose primary responsibility was to keep everyone in the conversation and in play."
>
> And Catholic lay people learned . . . "that virtually everything in the Church was questionable: doctrine, morals, the priesthood, the episcopate, the lot." Thus the impulse toward Cafeteria Catholicism got a decisive boost from the Truce of 1968: if the bishops and the Holy See were not going to defend seriously the Church's teaching on this matter, then picking-and-choosing in a supermarket of doctrinal and moral possibilities seemed, not simply all right, but actually

admirable—an exercise in maturity, as was often suggested at the time.[80]

"[S]o far as I have been able to discern," said Cardinal Lawrence Shehan, Archbishop of Baltimore, on the public dissent by priests from *Humanae Vitae,* "never in the recorded history of the Church has a solemn proclamation of a Pope been received by any group of Catholic people with so much disrespect and contempt."[81] That showing of contempt for Paul VI and *Humanae Vitae* was a revolution. The price of it was paid, not by the bugout clerics but by the Catholic people, especially students, who had no way of knowing that they were victims of a deceit, a fraud of nondisclosure. Consider a typical example:

"My education," said Minnesota educator Alyssa Bormes, "included four years of CCD and eight years of Catholic schools, including high school. There were a variety of teachers that we were exposed to; it was during the 70s and 80s and opinions varied greatly on Church teaching. . . . But *nothing* was ever taught about *Humanae Vitae.* When I read it the first time, it was breathtaking. Pope Paul VI had predicted my life. Why hadn't anyone spoken about it? It seemed there was a conspiracy of silence surrounding it. . . . In my mind, if the Church wasn't giving an argument, there must not be one. It must be some unimportant trifle and we need not pay attention to it. . . . I believed the only voice I heard—that of the world. Nothing will happen if you use contraception. The world was right, nothing did happen. My soul seemed to be nothing; my self worth was nothing; what men thought of me was nothing. And nothing happened. I didn't find what I was looking for; I got nothing back from the men; and there was nothing to show for all the 'fun.' My life was a shambles. . . . [W]orse than listening to the world [on] contraception, I also listened to the world [on] abortion. I am the mother of two

---

80   George Weigel, "The 'Truce of 1968,' Once Again," see www.dioceseofmarquette.org/upcarticle, May 17, 2006.
81   Quoted in Cardinal James Francis Stafford, "The Year of the Peirasmos—1968," www.catholicnewsagency.com.

dead children. These anniversaries haunt me as well: the dates of the children having been conceived, having died, the dates they should have been born, and the many birthdays that have passed without them. This year one of them should have graduated from college and next year the other. . . . Today, I read *Humanae Vitae* again. For me, the shocking thing today was the call for *Humanae Vitae* to be *taught!* The Church wasn't silent! Paul VI appealed to educators, public authorities, scientists, doctors and other medical professionals, husbands and wives, priests and bishops. In 1968 the Holy Father called these people to *teach*—to teach *Humanae Vitae.*[82] Would I have listened if I had been taught? I did listen, it was just that I was taught by the world. But I also heard the silence—and acted on it. If *Humanae Vitae* had been taught, would I have listened? I'll never know, but I would have loved the opportunity."[83]

It would be easy to marshal anecdotal evidence of the results of the bishops' failure to teach. In 2012, Pope Benedict offered to the American bishops a gentle but pointed summary: "Certainly we must acknowledge deficiencies in the catechesis of recent decades, which failed at times to communicate the rich heritage of Catholic teaching on marriage as a natural institution elevated by Christ to the dignity of a sacrament, the vocation of Christian spouses in society and in the Church, and in the practice of marital chastity."[84] That failure to teach is surely a decisive cause of the well documented—and appalling—decline in Catholic numbers and practice.

The Pew Research Religion and Public Life Project[85] reported on March 13, 2013, that "[a]bout a quarter (27%) of American Catholics called themselves 'strong' Catholics last year, down more than 15 points since the mid-1980s and among the lowest levels seen in the 38 years since strength of religious identity was first measured. . . . The share of all Catholics who say they attend Mass

---

82 See *HV*, nos. 22–31.
83 Alyssa Bormes, "Silence, then Nothing," *The Wanderer*, July 7, 2011.
84 Pope Benedict to American bishops, *Ad limina*, March 14, 2012.
85 www.pewforum.org/2013/03/13

at least once a week has dropped from 47% in 1974 to 24% in 2012; among 'strong' Catholics, it has fallen more than 30 points, from 85% in 1974 to 53% last year." When only 27% of American Catholics describe themselves as "strong" and only half (53%) of those "strong" Catholics go to Mass at least once a week, the influence of the pagan culture can be blamed. But not entirely. "If this doesn't, in one glaringly blinding snapshot, prove that the leadership of the Church in America is simply out to lunch and has been for decades . . . nothing does. . . . [I]t has taken 40 years for these numbers to plummet to their current all time low. This situation was inherited, not caused, by the current class of bishops [but] it is up to them to clean up the mess and that . . . by every single measure possible—is simply not happening."[86]

"The single most crucial need to stem this hemorrhage from the Catholic Faith," said Fr. John A. Hardon, S.J., "is for the Church's leaders to stand behind the Vicar of Christ in proclaiming the Church's two millennia of teaching that no marital act can be separated from its God-given purpose to conceive and procreate a child."[87]

Cardinal Dolan focused on *Humanae Vitae* in his admission that the bishops failed to teach. But that failure is more extensive than *Humanae Vitae*. "One cannot escape," said John Paul II, "the fact that more than in any other historical period, there is a breakdown in the process of handing on moral and religious values between generations."[88]

Every Sunday, opportunities have been missed. Dean Emeritus Jude Dougherty, of the School of Philosophy of the Catholic University of America, voiced a common lament of active Catholics: "From the pulpit," he asked, "when have you ever heard a sermon on any one of the Ten Commandments, the sacraments, or the virtues?" This cannot be blamed simply on parish priests. "It takes a genius, and few have talent," continues Dean

86 Michael Voris, *Vortex*, Aug. 22, 2013, www.Church.Militant.tv.
87 John A. Hardon, S.J., "Contraception: Fatal to the Faith and to Eternal Life," *Eternal Life*, April 19, 1999.
88 Pope John Paul II, *Address*, March 16, 2002.

Dougherty, "to make sense of the disparate biblical readings, which lend themselves to storybook repetition, rather than to the preaching of doctrine."[89]

The "breakdown in . . . handing on moral and religious values" is especially noticeable and harmful with respect to marriage and the family. "Sadly," said Bishop Kevin C. Rhoades, chairman of the USCCB Committee on Laity, Marriage, Family Life and Youth, "the majority of Catholics still do not know about church teachings on married love nor understand why the Church considers artificial contraception immoral. . . . This, tragically, is due to inconsistent education and formation since 1968. Over the last 30 years, we have been striving to correct the situation."[90] A Nationwide Bulletin Insert issued by the USCCB in the Summer of 2012 was refreshing in its unaccustomed clarity: "When a couple deliberately contracepts or sterilizes their sexual union, they change the meaning of their love and their relationship to God. . . . The impact of a contraceptive mentality is not isolated to individual couples. The widespread use of contraception impacts the entire culture, forming societies to be self-seeking, not welcoming to new life."

Truth in labeling requires that we admit candidly, with Cardinal Dolan, that for four decades and more the bishops "forfeited their chance to be a coherent moral voice." That admission is also a starting point, a foundation, for corrective action by all Catholics, bishops included. It took courage for the bishops to admit their dereliction and especially their appalling failure to teach the young. Catholics, whether they tell the pollsters that they are "strong" or not, know that they owe to the bishops, who are trying to make things right, their encouragement, support, and most of all, prayer. The stakes are high. As Father Hardon put it:

> I make bold to say that the Catholic Church, the real
> Roman Catholic Church, will survive only where her

89 Jude P. Dougherty, "The Holy Sacrifice of the Mass," *The Wanderer*, May 3, 2012, 4A.
90 www.ncronline.org/news/people, July 20-August 2, 2012.

bishops are courageous enough to proclaim what the followers of Christ have believed since apostolic times. But the bishops are frail human beings. They need, Lord how they need, the backing and support of the faithful under their care.[91]

---

91 John A. Hardon, S.J., "Contraception: Fatal to the Faith and to Eternal Life," *Eternal Life*, April 19, 1999.

PART IV. THE RESPONSE

13. TRUTH, TRUST AND PRAYER

No human sin can erase the mercy of God, or prevent him from unleashing all his triumphant power, if we only call upon him."—*Pope John Paul II*[1]

Humanae Vitae in Context

The teaching of the Church on marriage and the family is one of the Church's strongest weapons[2] because that teaching is part of something bigger. "The Christian faith," as John Paul II put it, "is not simply a set of propositions to be accepted with intellectual assent. Rather, faith is a lived knowledge of Christ, a living remembrance of his commandments and *a truth to be lived out.* . . . It entails a trusting abandonment to Christ."[3] The Catholic Church is "the Mystical Body of Christ. . . . 'We must accustom ourselves to see Christ Himself in the Church. For it is indeed Christ who lives in the Church, and through her teaches, governs and sanctifies.'"[4]

In his third encyclical, Benedict XVI said, "*Humanae Vitae* [locates] at the foundation of society the married couple, man and woman, who accept one another mutually, in distinction and complementarity; a couple, therefore, that is open to life. This is not a question of purely individual morality; *Humanae Vitae* indicates the

---

1   Pope John Paul II, *VS*, no. 118.
2   See Chapter 2.
3   *VS*, no. 88.
4   Pope Paul VI, *Ecclesiam Suam* (1964), nos. 30, 35, quoting Pope Pius XII, *Mystici Corporis* (1943).

strong links between life ethics and social ethics, ushering in a new area of magisterial teaching that has gradually been articulated in a series of documents, most recently John Paul II's Encyclical *Evangelium Vitae*. The Church forcefully maintains this link between life ethics and social ethics, fully aware that 'a society lacks solid foundations when . . . it asserts values such as the dignity of the person, justice and peace, but then . . . acts to the contrary by allowing or tolerating . . . ways in which human life is devalued and violated, especially where it is weak or marginalized.'"[5]

Humanae Vitae is not some narrow mandate for marital behavior. It is part of "the Church's social doctrine," described by Benedict as "a set of fundamental guidelines [which] need to be addressed in . . . dialogue with all those seriously concerned for humanity and the world in which we live."[6] The *Compendium of the Social Doctrine of the Church*, published in 2004 by the Pontifical Council on Justice and Peace, summarized concisely the teaching of *Humanae Vitae* in its section entitled, "The family is the sanctuary of life."[7]

Speak the Truth—in Detail

In this time for choosing between truth and the lie, a true witness requires that we speak the truth with clarity as well as charity. Truth can have an impact beyond what we know. Cardinal Eduoard Gagnon described a conversation he had with John Paul II: "[T]he Holy Father . . . told me, 'error makes its way because truth is not taught. We must teach the truth . . . not attacking the ones who teach errors because that would never end—they are too numerous. We have to teach the truth.' He told me truth has a grace attached to it. The truth may not immediately enter in the mind and heart of those to whom we talk, but the grace of God is there and at the time they need it, God will open their heart and

---

5   *C in V*, no. 15.
6   *DCE*, no. 27.
7   *Compendium*, nos. 232–33.

they will accept it. He said, error does not have a grace accompanying it."[8]

An effective witness to Truth will affirm that God is Love,[9] that God is *Rich in Mercy*,[10] and that "The Redeemer of man, Jesus Christ, is the center of the universe and of history."[11] "In Jesus Christ," said Benedict XVI, "a great light emerged for us, *the* great Light; we cannot put it under a bushel basket, we must set it on a lampstand so that it will give light to all who are in the house (cf. Mt 5:15).[12]

Truth, with a capital T, is not an abstraction but a Person, Jesus Christ, who speaks to us through his Vicar on earth. "We need to bring the *Gospel of Life*," said John Paul, "to the heart of every man and woman and to make it penetrate every part of society. This involves above all proclaiming *the core* of this Gospel. It is the proclamation of the living God who is close to us, who calls us to profound communion with himself and awakens in us the certain hope of eternal life."[13]

This "involves making clear all *the consequences* of this Gospel. These can be summed up as follows: human life, as a gift of God, is sacred and inviolable. . . . [P]rocured abortion and euthanasia are absolutely unacceptable. . . . [H]uman life . . . must be protected with loving concern. The meaning of life is found in giving and receiving love, and in this light human sexuality and procreation reach their true and full significance. Love also gives meaning to suffering and death; despite the mystery which surrounds them, they can become saving events. Respect for life requires that science and technology should always be at the service of man and his integral development. Society as a whole must respect, defend and promote the dignity of every human person, at every moment . . . of that person's life. To be truly a people at

8   *Lay Witness*, March 1, 1990, 6.
9   Pope Benedict XVI, *Deus Caritas Est* (2006).
10 Pope John Paul II, *Dives in Misericordia* (1980).
11 Pope John Paul II, *Redemptor Hominis* (1979), no. 1.
12 Address to the Roman Curia, Dec. 21, 2007.
13 *EV*, nos. 80–81.

the service of life, we must propose these truths constantly and courageously."[14]

Pope Francis followed that prescription when he told Catholic obstetricians and gynecologists in Sardinia: "The Lord is also counting on you to spread 'the gospel of life." "Every child," he said, "condemned unjustly to being aborted, bears the face of Jesus Christ. . . . And every elderly person, even if he is ill or at the end of his days, bears the face of Jesus Christ. They cannot be discarded, as the 'culture of waste' suggests! They cannot be thrown away!" The Holy Father noted that "concern for human life in its totality has become in recent years a real priority for the Church's Magisterium, especially for the most defenseless; i.e., the disabled, the sick, the newborn, children, the elderly."[15]

Pray: The Eucharist and Mary

Two effective ways to call upon God are through the Eucharist, the "Sacrament of sacraments,"[16] and through "Mary, Mother of Christ, Mother of the Church."[17]

Eucharistic Adoration[18]

"How I should like all the parishes of the world to be open to Perpetual Adoration of the Eucharist!" John Paul II said in 1993.[19] Over the past two decades, "there has been a striking resurgence in the practice of exposition . . . holy hours of adoration and perpetual Eucharistic adoration."[20]

14 *Ibid.*, nos. 81–82.
15 *L'Osservatore Romano*, Sept. 25, 2013; Catholic News Agency, Sept. 20, 2013.
16 CCC, nos. 1211, 1322 et seq.
17 CCC, no. 963.
18 See generally, John Paul II's *Ecclesia de Eucharistia* (2003).
19 Alberto Pacini, "Be 'Archangels' of his Eucharistic Kingship!" *L'Osservatore Romano*, May 30, 2007.
20 Cardinal Avery Dulles, "Truly, Really and Substantially," *Our Sunday Visitor*, May 29, 2005.

How does Eucharistic Adoration relate to the assault on freedom by the secular State? "Kneeling before the Eucharist," said Benedict, "is a profession of freedom: those who bow to Jesus cannot and must not prostrate themselves before any earthly authority, only before God or before the Most Blessed Sacrament because we know and believe that the one true God is present in it, the God who created the world and so loved it that he gave his Only Begotten Son (cf. Jn 3:16)."[21] "The time you spend with Jesus in the Blessed Sacrament," said Blessed Mother Teresa of Calcutta, "will help bring about an everlasting peace on earth."[22]

Mary

> God has never made and formed but one enmity; but it is an irreconcilable one, which shall endure and grow even to the end. It is between Mary, His worthy Mother, and the devil—between the children and servants of the Blessed Virgin, and the children and tools of Lucifer. The most terrible of all the enemies which God has set up against the devil is His holy Mother Mary.[23]

After he was shot in Saint Peter's Square by an assailant on May 13, 1981, John Paul II attributed his survival to Our Lady of Fatima. Our Lady had appeared to three young children in Fatima, Portugal, on May 13, 1917, and each month thereafter until October 13, 1917. The Pope journeyed to Fatima to offer thanks to Mary for his survival of the attempt on his life. He said in his homily at Fatima, on May 13, 1982, "while the message of Our Lady of Fatima is a motherly one, it is also strong and decisive. It sounds severe. It sounds like John the Baptist speaking on the banks of the Jordan. It invites to repentance. It gives a warning. It calls to prayer. It recommends the Rosary. The

21 Homily, May 22, 2008.
22 Missionaries of the Blessed Sacrament, *Newsletter*, no. 58 (Sept. 2002).
23 St. Louis de Montfort, *True Devotion to Mary* (1941), 30–31.

message is addressed to every human being . . . [T]he . . . call to repentance and conversion, uttered in the Mother's message, remains ever relevant. It is still more relevant than it was [in 1917]. It is still more urgent."[24]

Devotion to Mary, the Mother of God, is rising.[25] "Mary prays," said Pope Francis, "and she teaches us to have complete trust in God and in his mercy. This is the power of prayer! . . . Every day through Mary let us carry our entire life to God's heart! Knock at the door of God's heart!"[26]

Trust by Faith

In merely political terms, the Total State looks like a winner. And the civilized order based on reason and faith looks like a loser. Not so. "Let us be certain," said St. Maximilian Kolbe, "that God permits everything in view of a greater blessing."[27]

"Mary," said Pope Francis, "teaches us that God does not abandon us; he can do great things even with our weaknesses."[28] Fr. Walter J. Ciszek, S.J., is a case in point.

Born in 1904 in Pennsylvania as the seventh of thirteen children of Polish immigrant parents, Walter Ciszek inherited toughness from his coal miner/saloon keeper father and religious training from his mother. He entered the Jesuits in 1928. In 1939, he entered the Soviet Union as a clandestine priest.[29] He was arrested and spent 23 years in Soviet prisons before his release in 1963 in exchange for two Soviet spies. During the first of his five years in Moscow's Lubianka Prison, interrogators pressed him to confess that he was a Vatican spy.[30]

24 Pope John Paul II, Homily, May 13, 1982.
25 See Pope John Paul II, *Redemptoris Mater* (1987).
26 Pope Francis, Homily, Sept. 22, 2013; *L'Osservatore Romano*, Sept. 25, 2013; Catholic News Agency, Sept. 22, 2013.
27 *Writings of Maximilian Kolbe*, 1205.
28 *L'Osservatore Romano*, Sept. 25, 2013.
29 See generally, Walter J. Ciszek, S.J., *With God in Russia* (1964), reprinted in 1997; *He Leadeth Me* (1973), reprinted in 1995.
30 Quotations are from He Leadeth Me, chapters 5–7.

Fr. Ciszek steeled himself by prayer to resist the pressure. He was determined to die rather than give in. When the interrogator reached the end of the line, he put before Fr. Ciszek the false confessions and gave the ultimatum: "If you don't sign those pages, I can sign one right here and you'll be dead before the sun sets!"[31] Fr. Ciszek, the unbreakable tough guy—caved. His surrender was complete. "I picked up the pen and began to sign. As I signed the pages, largely without reading them, I began to burn with shame and guilt. I was totally broken, totally humiliated."[32] Back in his cell, he was "tormented by feelings of defeat, failure and guilt."[33] "I felt guilty because I . . . had asked for God's help but had really believed in my own ability to avoid evil and meet every challenge."[34]

Fr. Ciszek was sentenced to fifteen years of hard labor but was kept for four more years in Lubianka while the interrogators pressed him to become a Soviet spy in the Vatican. He sank into feelings of "despondency and despair."[35] Then he went from "thoughts of our Lord and his agony in the garden" to what "I can only call . . . a conversion experience. . . . I was brought to make this perfect act of faith, this act of complete self-abandonment to his will, of total trust in his love and concern for me and his desire to sustain and protect me, by the experience of a complete despair of my own powers and abilities. . . . I knew I could no longer trust myself, and it seemed sensible then to trust totally in God. . . . I saw all things now as coming from the hands of God. . . . [W]hatever he chose to send me in the future, I would accept."[36]

After many interrogations, the interrogator finally asked him to sign an agreement to serve as a Soviet spy in Rome. Fr. Ciszek refused. The interrogator "threatened me with immediate

31 *He Leadeth Me*, 66.
32 *Ibid.*
33 *Ibid.*, 67.
34 *Ibid.*, 68.
35 *Ibid.*, 75.
36 *Ibid.*, 76–80.

execution. I felt no fear at all. I think I smiled."[37] Fr. Ciszek left that room, not to receive a bullet in the head, but to begin his fifteen-year sentence.

We are called, of course, to use our talents on behalf of the Culture of Life. But, as we learn from Fr. Ciszek, the success of those efforts depends absolutely on faith and trust in God. Fr. Ciszek, a very tough guy, nevertheless failed his test because he trusted in Walter Ciszek rather than in Jesus Christ. And we will fail if we make that same mistake. Fr. Ciszek offers us the certainty that "just as surely as man begins to trust in his own abilities, so surely has he taken that first step on the road to ultimate failure. And the greatest grace God can give such a man is to send him a trial he cannot bear with his own powers—and then sustain him with his grace so he may endure to the end and be saved."[38]

Fr. Ciszek's bottom line: What God wants, especially in times of adversity or danger, is "an act of total trust," demanding "absolute faith: faith in God's existence, in his providence, in his concern for the minutest detail, in his power to sustain me, and in his love protecting me."[39]

Excita, Domine. . . .

In his Christmas address to the Roman Curia in 2010, Pope Benedict XVI invoked repeatedly the Advent prayer, "*Excita, Domine, potentiam tuam, et veni.*" "Rouse, O Lord, your power and come." That invocation, he said, was "formulated as the Roman Empire was in decline. . . . The sun was setting over an entire world. . . . There was no power in sight that could put a stop to this decline. All the more insistent, then, was the invocation of the power of God: the plea that he might come and protect his people from all these threats.

37 *Ibid.*, 81.
38 *Ibid.*, 71.
39 *Ibid.*, 77. The case for Fr. Ciszek's canonization is underway. See Father Walter Ciszek Prayer League, 231 N. Jardin Street, Shenandoah, PA 17976-1642. Email: fwccenter@verizon.net; website: http://www.ciszek.org.

"*Excita, Domine, potentiam tuam, et veni.* Today, too, we have many reasons to associate ourselves with this Advent prayer of the Church. . . . [M]oral consensus is collapsing, consensus without which juridical and political structures cannot function. . . .

"*Excita*—the prayer recalls the cry addressed to the Lord who was sleeping in the disciples' storm-tossed boat as it was close to sinking. When [he] had calmed the storm, he rebuked the disciples for their little faith. . . . He wanted to say: it was your faith that was sleeping. He will say the same thing to us. Our faith too is asleep. Let us ask him, then, to wake us from the sleep of a faith grown tired, and to restore to that faith the power to move mountains—that is, to justly order the affairs of the world."[40]

This is a great time for us to be here. We have the Truth, in the Person, Jesus Christ. Our "nuclear weapon," however, is prayer—for our country and for our Church, especially through the intercession of Mary, the mother of Life. As John Paul II wrote in a letter to U.S. bishops in 1993: "America needs much prayer—lest it lose its soul."[41]

40 Pope Benedict XVI, *Address*, Dec. 20, 2010.
41 Pope John Paul II, Letter to the U.S. Bishops, June 11, 1993; 38 *The Pope Speaks* (1993), 374, 376.

INDEX

* Where a name or subject is mentioned or discussed on consecutive pages in the text, the first such page is stated in the Index.

Biography

Charles E. Rice is Professor Emeritus at Notre Dame Law School and Chairman of the "Bellarmine Forum. He was born in 1931 and attended the College of the Holy Cross (B.A.), Boston College Law School (J.D.), and New York University School of Law (L.L.M.; J.S.D.). Before joining the Notre Dame faculty in 1969, he practiced law in New York and taught at New York University and Fordham Law School. He is the author of numerous books on constitutional and jurisprudential issues. He is a LtCol (Ret.) in the Marine Corps Reserve and from 1970 to 2010 was an assistant coach of the Notre Dame Boxing Club. He and his wife, Mary, have ten children and forty-one grandchildren and live in Mishawaka, Indiana.